GREAT MILITARY LEADERS
of the 20TH Century

Douglas MacArthur
Mao Zedong
George S. Patton
John J. Pershing
Erwin J.E. Rommel
H. Norman Schwarzkopf

GREAT MILITARY LEADERS
of the 20ᵀᴴ Century

MAO
ZEDONG

LOUISE CHIPLEY SLAVICEK

INTRODUCTION BY
CASPAR W. WEINBERGER

SERIES CONSULTING EDITOR
EARLE RICE JR.

CHELSEA HOUSE
PUBLISHERS
A Haights Cross Communications Company

FRONTIS: **Portrait of Mao**

DEDICATION: **For Krista Ann Slavicek**

CHELSEA HOUSE PUBLISHERS

VP, NEW PRODUCT DEVELOPMENT Sally Cheney
DIRECTOR OF PRODUCTION Kim Shinners
CREATIVE MANAGER Takeshi Takahashi
MANUFACTURING MANAGER Diann Grasse

STAFF FOR MAO ZEDONG

EXECUTIVE EDITOR Lee Marcott
PRODUCTION ASSISTANT Megan Emery
PICTURE RESEARCHER Sarah Bloom
SERIES & COVER DESIGNER Keith Trego
LAYOUT 21st Century Publishing and Communications, Inc.

A Haights Cross Communications ✦ Company

http://www.chelseahouse.com

First Printing

1 3 5 7 9 8 6 4 2

Library of Congress Cataloging-in-Publication Data

Slavicek, Louise Chipley, 1956-
  Mao Zedong / by Louise Chipley Slavicek.
    p. cm. -- (Great military leaders of the 20th century)
Summary: A biography of Chinese leader Mao Zedong, discussing the
battles that helped shape him and reasons behind his popularity among
his countrymen. Includes bibliographical references and index.
Audience: "Age: 12+."
  ISBN 0-7910-7407-2 (Hardcover)
 1. Mao, Zedong, 1893-1976--Military leadership--Juvenile literature. 2.
China--History--1949-1976--Juvenile literature. [1. Mao, Zedong, 1893-
1976. 2. Heads of state. 3. China--History--20th century.] I. Title. II.
Series.
DS778.M3S58 2003
951.05'092--dc21

2003006929

TABLE OF CONTENTS

INTRODUCTION

by Caspar W. Weinberger

At a time when it is ever more apparent that the world will need skilled and bold military leaders, it is both appropriate and necessary that school history courses include studies of great military leaders.

Democracies, for the most part, are basically not greatly interested in military leadership or military matters in general. Fortunately, in the United States we have sufficient interest and volunteers for military service so that we can maintain and staff a very strong military with volunteers—people who want to serve.

That is very fortunate indeed for us. Volunteers and those who decide of their own free will that they want to be in the military are, generally speaking, easier to train, and to retain in the services, and their morale is markedly higher than that of conscripts. Furthermore, the total effect of a draft, based on our Vietnam experience, can be very bad—indeed it can polarize the country as a whole.

One of the best ways of ensuring that we will continue to have enough volunteers in the future is to study the great accomplishments of our past military leaders—the small group of leaders and others who contributed so much to our past greatness and our present strength.

Not all of these leaders have been Americans, but the

example that all of them set are well worth studying in our schools. Of the six military leaders chosen by Chelsea House's "Great Military Leaders of the 20th Century," I had the privilege of serving under and with two.

In World War II, after two years of volunteer service in the infantry at home and in the Pacific, I was transferred from the 41st Infantry Division then in New Guinea, to General Douglas MacArthur's intelligence staff in Manila, in the Philippines. One of my assignments was to prepare drafts of the general's daily communiqué to other theatre commanders around the world. This required seeing all of the major military cable and intelligence information, and digesting the most important items for his daily report to the other war theatres of the world. It also required a familiarity with our plans to carry the war to the enemy as soon as sufficient strength had been transferred to our theatre from Europe.

The invasion of Japan toward which all the planning was aiming would have been a very difficult and costly operation. Most of the tentative plans called for landing our force on one of the southern Japanese islands, and another force on Honshu, north of Tokyo.

We know that Japan's troops would have fought fiercely and very skillfully once their homeland was invaded. In fact, all of our plans forecast that we would lose virtually all of the first two U.S. divisions that landed. That was one of the main reasons that President Harry Truman concluded we had to use the atomic bomb. That ended the war, and all landings taken in Japan were peaceful and unopposed.

Many years later, when I was secretary of defense under President Ronald Reagan, a part of my duties was to recommend generals and admirals for various U.S. and NATO regional commands. Fulfilling this duty led me to interview several possible candidates for the post of commander in chief of our Central Command, which had jurisdiction over our many military activities in the Middle East.

My strong recommendation, accepted by the president, was that he name General H. Norman Schwarzkopf to lead the Central Command. A short time later, General Schwarzkopf led our forces in that region to the great military victory of the Gulf War.

General MacArthur and General Schwarzkopf shared many of the same qualities. Both were very experienced army officers tested by many widely different conditions all over the world. Both were calm, resolute, and inspirational leaders. Both were superb military planners and developers of complex and very large-scale military operations. Both achieved great military successes; both had the best interest of all our troops at heart; and both were leaders in the best sense of the word. They both had the ability and skills necessary to work with military and civilian leaders of our allies and friends in all parts of the globe.

It is vitally important for our future as a democracy, a superpower and a country whose strengths have helped save freedom and peace, that our children and our schools know far more about these leaders and countless others like them who serve the cause of peace with freedom so well and so faithfully. Their lives and the lives of others like them will be a great inspiration for us and for later generations who need to know what America at its best can accomplish.

The other military leaders whose lives are presented in this series include a German, General Erwin Rommel, and the former Communist China leader, Mao Zedong.

General Rommel won many preliminary battles in the desert war of World War II before losing the decisive battle of El Alamein. He had to develop and execute his tactics for desert fighting under conditions not previously experienced by him or his troops. He also became one of the masters of the art of tank warfare.

Mao Zedong had to train, develop, arm, and deploy huge numbers of Chinese soldiers to defeat the organized and experienced forces of Chiang Kai-shek's Nationalist government. He accomplished this and, in comparatively short time, won the military victories that transformed his country.

Both of these generals had to learn, very quickly, the new tactics needed to cope with rapidly changing conditions. In short, they had to be flexible, inventive, and willing and able to fight against larger opposing forces and in unfamiliar environments.

This whole series demonstrates that great military success requires many of the qualities and skills required for success in other fields of endeavor. Military history is indeed a vital part of the whole story of mankind, and one of the best ways of studying that history is to study the lives of those who succeeded by their leadership in this vital field.

CASPAR W. WEINBERGER
CHAIRMAN, *FORBES* INC
MARCH 2003

★   ★   ★

CASPAR W. WEINBERGER was the fifteenth U.S. secretary of defense, serving under President Ronald Reagan from 1981 to 1987, longer than any previous defense secretary except Robert McNamara (served 1961–1968). Weinberger is also an author who has written books about his experiences in the Reagan administration and about U.S. military capabilities.

1

From the Barrel of a Gun: October 1, 1949

On October 1, 1949, an excited throng gathered before the Gate of Heavenly Peace (Tiananmen) in Beijing, China, to witness the birth of a new epoch in their homeland's long history. The crowd let out a great cheer as Mao Zedong, chairman of the Communist Party of China and the new leader of the Chinese state, stepped out onto a balcony high on the towering gate.

Clearing his throat, Mao began to speak. He reminded his listeners of how their ancient homeland had been exploited and bullied by foreign powers for more than a century and was only now emerging from three devastating years of full-scale civil war between his Communist forces and the Nationalist armies of Chiang Kaishek. Thanking all those Chinese who had "laid down their lives in the many struggles against domestic and foreign enemies" during the course of the past tumultuous century, Mao assured his audience that the humiliation, disunity, and violence that had plagued China for so long were over at last.[1]

"We, the 475 million Chinese people, have stood up," he proclaimed, "and our future is infinitely bright."[2]

When Mao announced the establishment of the People's Republic of China—the new state that would lead the Chinese people into their "infinitely bright" future—there was an eruption of clapping, shouting, and jubilation from the square below. Over and over again, the crowd yelled, "Long live the People's Republic!" "Long live the Communist Party!" and loudest and of all, "Long live Chairman Mao! A long, long, life to Chairman Mao!"

Indeed, it probably would have been impossible for anyone in Tiananmen Square that autumn day to conceive of this hopeful new era in Chinese history without Chairman Mao. For more than two decades, Mao had led the communists in their fight against their chief internal foe—Chiang Kaishek and his nationalists—pausing from the bitter struggle with Chiang only to help drive the Japanese army from China during the Sino-Japanese War (1937–1945).

Political power, Mao bluntly declared early in his long struggle for control of China, flows "from the barrel of the gun."[3] On October 1, 1949, as Mao announced the founding of the People's Republic after more than two decades of armed conflict with domestic and foreign foes, it seemed that his dictum regarding the inextricable bond between political and military might was being

October 1, 1949, marked a pivotal point in China's history. With Beijing's Tiananmen Square filled with excited onlookers, Communist Party Chairman Mao Zedong proclaimed the founding of the Peoples' Republic of China. Mao's resourcefulness in reaching that goal proved him to be one of the century's most important military leaders.

proved true. Mao's successful campaign to attain supreme political power in China for himself and the Communist Party he dominated, most scholars concur, owed a great deal to his remarkable skill and tenacity as a military leader. With virtually no help from outside allies and little formal military training, Mao managed to transform a ragtag peasant band into a well-disciplined and motivated army of millions, as well as devise an effective guerrilla-warfare strategy for it to resist larger, better-equipped adversaries.

From 1949 until his death in 1976 at the age of 82, Mao Zedong would dominate the new communist state that his adept military leadership had helped to create. Chairman Mao was the key figure behind every important military and political path that the People's Republic followed during those three decades: its early alliance with the Soviet Union and the eventual collapse of that coalition; its deep involvement in the Korean War and more limited role in the Vietnamese conflict; its reliance on the national army to promote—and then to rein in—the terror of the notorious Cultural Revolution; and finally, its startling rapprochement with a long-standing and powerful enemy, the United States.

Mao Zedong will long be remembered as one of the twentieth century's most resourceful military and political leaders. Unquestionably, he was also one of its most influential. For as Mao was building and maintaining his considerable personal power within China, he was also making his once weak and divided homeland into a major global power and transforming forever the lives of billions of his compatriots.

2

Finding a Road:
The Early Years: 1893–1921

Mao Zedong was born in the tiny village of Shaoshan in south-central China on December 26, 1893. Mao made his appearance in the world at a painful time in his homeland's long history, as China confronted grave threats to its economic and political independence from abroad and weak leadership at home. Traditionally, the Chinese had viewed their vast country as the "Middle Kingdom"—the very heart of the civilized world. By the late 1800s, however, faced with the modernized armies and technological expertise of the imperialist West, the once proud Middle Kingdom had been humiliated and demoralized.

A TROUBLED LAND: THE CHINA OF MAO'S YOUTH

After years of self-imposed isolation from the outside world, during the half-century preceding Mao Zedong's birth China found itself besieged by western merchants and governments determined to carve out "spheres of influence" for themselves in Asia's largest and most populous country. As the nineteenth century progressed, the ineffectual emperors of China's ruling family, the Qing Dynasty, made only feeble efforts to halt the growing exploitation of their country's economy and natural resources by England, Russia, and other foreign powers. Intimidated by their modernized armies, China's leaders allowed the intruders to set up their own courts of law within the empire and evade Chinese justice; control naval stations, railroad, and mining rights in a number of vital areas; and exact sweeping trade privileges.

When Mao was still an infant, China's chief Asian rival—Japan—took advantage of its neighbor's weakness by invading Korea, a longtime Chinese tributary. By 1895, Japan's modernized army had managed to conquer not only Korea but also Taiwan, which China had governed for centuries. Five years later, the Middle Kingdom's national pride received another blow when the Boxer Rebellion, a violent crusade to expel all foreigners from China, was crushed with brutal efficiency by an international army including Japanese, American, and European troops.

The poverty and backwardness of China's predominantly rural populace added greatly to the country's weakness in the face of its foreign rivals. At the turn of the twentieth century, China was far less industrialized or urbanized than Japan or any of its western rivals. As had been the case for countless centuries, the vast majority of Chinese were illiterate peasants who barely managed to eke a living out of the land. Compelled to rent their fields

For centuries, China's emperors (whose history and lifestyle is reflected in this engraving) had pursued a course of isolation. Western powers—including England, France, Russia, and the United States—exploited this position, using their technologically superior armies to bully China into giving up control of its natural resources, railroads, trade, and even courts to Western powers.

at prohibitive rates from a small group of wealthy landlords, they were perpetually in debt, with scant hope of ever improving their economic situation. Consequently, social unrest was rampant among the Chinese peasantry, especially in Mao's home province of Hunan, where land rents were notoriously high. During Mao's childhood, thousands of angry peasants descended on the provincial capital of Changsha, demanding food after drought and famine struck Hunan. Their protest, however, ended quickly when government forces opened fire on the marchers.

A DEFIANT SON: ESCAPING SHAOSHAN

Between the debt-ridden masses that constituted the bulk of China's population and the minute class of rich landlords that stood at the top of the country's rural hierarchy stood another group, often referred to as the middle peasants. These middling peasants typically possessed a few acres of land, which they tilled with the help of a hired hand or two. It was into this small and relatively prosperous class of peasants that Mao Zedong was born in 1893.

Mao's father, Rensheng, had pulled himself up from the lower to the middle ranks of the peasantry by enlisting in the provincial army at age 16, then carefully saving his pay until he could buy a plot of land back in his native village of Shaoshan. By hard work and thrift, Rensheng managed to not only expand his farmland but also branch off into grain trading, purchasing rice from his neighbors and then transporting it to a nearby city for resale at a much higher price. By the time Mao was born, Rensheng owned over two acres of rice paddy and a house so spacious that Mao, even after two brothers and a sister arrived on the scene, had his own bedroom—a rare luxury for a Shaoshan youngster.

When Mao was eight years old, Rensheng sent him to the village primary school to learn the fundamentals of reading and writing and to study the ancient Chinese classics, particularly the writings of the sixth-century B.C. scholar Confucius, whose ethical teachings had long dominated all levels of Chinese education. Although the tuition was costly by village standards—about the equivalent of six months' pay for a field hand—Rensheng, who was barely literate himself, wanted his first-born to be capable of composing letters and maintaining accurate accounts for the family business.

For the next five years, Mao attended school during the day, then assisted his father in the fields and with the book-keeping each evening. When Mao was 13, Rensheng, having concluded that his son required no further book learning, pulled him out of school to work full-time on the farm. A year later Rensheng announced that Mao was ready to marry and that he had picked out a suitable bride for his eldest son. In accordance with Chinese tradition, the young woman would move into her new husband's home, providing Mao's family with a much-needed extra pair of hands in the house and fields.

Although Chinese parents customarily arranged mar-riages for their teenage children, Mao refused to go along with his father's plans. Mao's revolt against Rensheng's authority was daring. Chinese fathers demanded—and generally received—strict obedience from their sons, for respect toward parents was a central tenet of the Confucian ethical system that had pervaded Chinese education and life for centuries. By this time, however, Mao had become resolved to escape from not only his father's controlling ways but his native village as well. Consequently, he was not about to permit himself to be dragged into a marriage that would serve only to bind him to a lifetime of drudgery within the cramped confines of Shaoshan. Mao had other plans for his future.

Mao wanted to go back to school—and not just any school. He wanted to attend a modern school that empha-sized western learning rather than the age-old Chinese classics that dominated the curriculum at his village school. Years later, Mao linked his determination to leave Shaoshan and continue his education to a book he borrowed from a cousin, *Words of Warning to an Affluent Age*. In the book, Mao learned for the first time of China's humiliating weakness before the demands of the modernized western powers. Warning that China was in grave peril of losing its political independence altogether, the author argued that the Middle Kingdom must embrace western technological innovations such as the railroad, telegraph, and factory system before it was too late.

Mao was shocked by what he learned regarding China's declining power in *Words of Warning,* for little news of the outside world reached secluded Shaoshan. Soon after reading *Words of Warning*, Mao was lent another disturbing work describing his homeland's diminishing international status, "The Dismemberment of China." This pamphlet detailed events from the last two decades with which Mao was completely unfamiliar, including Japan's colonization of Taiwan and Korea; France's military incursions into Indochina (Vietnam, Laos, and Cambodia), a region formerly dominated by China; and Britain's annexation of Burma, another one-time Chinese tributary. The book made such a deep impression on Mao that almost 30 years later he could still recite the author's opening sentence verbatim: "Alas, China will be subjugated!" After finishing the pamphlet, he recalled, "I felt depressed about the future of my country and began to realize that it was the duty of all the people to help save it."[4]

Determined to do his part to rescue his faltering homeland, Mao set out to obtain the sort of "modern" education the authors of *Words of Warning* and "The Dismemberment of China" urged on their readers as a means of meeting the threats posed to China by its western (or in Japan's case, westernized) rivals. Like many of his generation, Mao had become convinced that China must make use of the latest western political, social, and scientific ideas and practices—at least in the short run—if the Middle Kingdom was to be restored to its former glory.

Although Mao's father remained staunchly opposed to

By the late 1800s, a weak Chinese leadership had allowed Western powers to carve out great spheres of influence within China, as this cartoon shows. Growing up in this environment, the young Mao Zedong realized the importance of regaining national strength and pride for China, free from foreign exploitation.

his son's scheme for continuing his education, when Mao was 16, a sympathetic uncle arranged for the boy to attend a higher primary school that emphasized western learning in neighboring Xiangxiang county. After borrowing money from relatives to cover his tuition and living expenses, Mao set off on the 15-mile journey to his new school—his first-ever foray out of Shaoshan.

At the higher primary school in Xiangxiang, Mao studied natural science, world history, geography, and other "modern" subjects never dreamt of in Shaoshan's one-room schoolhouse. Military history, including the exploits of such western war heroes as George Washington and Napoleon Bonaparte, particularly captivated him.

Although many of Mao's classmates came from more prosperous families than his own and snubbed him for his shabby clothing and uncouth manners, Mao thrived in his new school, immersing himself in his studies and earning the respect of his teachers. By the summer of 1911, Mao's instructors thought the 17-year-old was ready to move on to the next step in his education—secondary school. Soon Mao was on a river steamer bound for Changsha, home to a well-regarded secondary school for students from Xiangxiang County. This time Mao had the support of his father, whose friends had convinced him that a secondary education would enable his eldest child to obtain a good job and bring honor to the family name.

PATRIOT AND SOLDIER: JOINING THE REPUBLICAN REVOLUTION

As it turned out, Mao spent only a few weeks at his new school. On October 10, 1911, a rebellion against the Qing dynasty broke out in Wuchang in central China. From there, with the backing of much of the imperial army, the uprising was able to spread rapidly through the central and southern regions of the country, including Hunan province.

The rebellion of 1911—or the Republican Revolution, as it became known—drew its inspiration from the modernizing republican movement of Dr. Sun Yatsen. Eventually, Sun's followers formed the Nationalist Party (NP) or Guomindang. The Republican Revolution thrilled Mao, who like many of his compatriots had come to despise the feeble Qin regime and found much to admire in Sun's goals of freeing China from foreign intrusion and establishing a strong national government based on western-style democracy.

Anxious to further the Republican cause, Mao dropped out of school and enlisted in the revolutionary forces. Although Mao spent a total of six months in the army, he saw no fighting. Assigned to garrison duty in Changsha, Mao passed his days doing chores for officers and writing letters home for the illiterate workers and peasants who comprised the bulk of his regiment.

By the spring of 1912, it seemed that the Republican Revolution had succeeded. The emperor had abdicated and China was now officially a republic, with the rebels' top military commander, Yuan Shikai, as president. (Although Sun Yatsen briefly held the presidency of the republic in January 1912, the following month Sun stepped down in favor of Yuan as part of a deal he struck with the general. In return for the presidency, Yuan promised to establish a parliament whose members would be elected by popular vote, in keeping with Sun's political principles.) "Thinking the revolution was over," Mao later recalled, "I resigned from the army and decided to return to my books."[5]

STUDENT AND POLITICAL ACTIVIST:
BUILDING A STRONGER CHINA

Racked by indecision and restlessness during the months following his discharge, Mao drifted from one educational institution to another in Changsha, trying law school, business school, and police school in turn. Finally, after a brief period of self-guided study during which he explored the writings of such western thinkers as Adam Smith and Charles Darwin, in 1913 Mao decided to enroll in the Hunan Normal School, a teacher-training college.

Mao remained at the Normal School for five years,

graduating in 1918 at the age of 25. During his years there, Mao, who had never encountered a single newspaper in Shaoshan or Xiangxiang, became an avid newspaper reader. From the newspapers, he learned about World War I (1914–1918), in which the Allies (principally France, England, Russia, the United States, and Japan) battled the Central Powers (Germany, Austria-Hungary, and Turkey). He also learned about dismaying events taking place in his own country, events that led him and many of his compatriots to conclude that the Republican Revolution had degenerated into a dismal failure.

By 1918, it was painfully clear that China was neither stronger nor more democratic since the Republican Revolution of 1911. The parliamentary elections promised to Sun Yatsen by Yuan Shikai had taken place, but when the Nationalists won at the polls, Yuan banned the Nationalist Party and forced Sun into exile. Yuan's death a few years later in 1916 caused a national power vacuum, with one province after another falling under the control of warlords (military strongmen), who formed their own private armies. A central government of sorts remained in the capital city of Beijing, but it retained little actual authority.

Mao was particularly concerned that China's political chaos made the country more vulnerable than ever to foreign intruders. Determined to do what he could to aid his struggling homeland, Mao started a study group in Changsha to discuss how China could remake itself as a modern and unified power. Mao's inspiration for the group was the radical magazine *New Youth,* which advocated sweeping social and political reforms in China. In 1917, Mao himself wrote an article for *New Youth* reflecting his grave concerns regarding China's future. In his article, Mao extolled physical education and the promotion of a martial spirit among the masses as a means of building a strong China capable of resisting foreign encroachment.

Mao, who engaged regularly in strenuous exercise, particularly distance swimming, wrote:

> Our nation is wanting in strength. The military spirit has not been encouraged. The physical condition of the population deteriorates daily. . . . If this state continues, our weakness will increase further. . . . If our bodies are not strong, we will be afraid as soon as we see enemy soldiers, and then how can we attain our goals and make ourselves respected?[6]

COMMUNIST PARTY MEMBER: FINDING A ROAD

Soon after graduating from Hunan Normal School, Mao decided to follow his teacher, Yang Changji, to Beijing, where Yang had obtained a professorship at prestigious Beijing University. With Yang's help, Mao found a job as a clerical worker at the university library. However, Mao was disappointed in his new position, for although he tried to strike up conversations about politics or culture with the scholars who passed by his desk, those important men made it abundantly clear that they had no time to waste on a lowly library assistant.

In the spring of 1919, Mao returned to Changsha to take a part-time teaching position at a primary school. On May 4, just a few weeks after Mao's departure from Beijing, the city's students took to the streets en masse under the leadership of Chen Duxiu, the editor of *New Youth* and an acquaintance of Mao's. They were protesting the decision of World War I's Allied victors to grant Chinese territory held by Germany to Japan instead of returning it to China, and the weakness of the Beijing government in allowing this outrage. In time, the student demonstrations and the nationwide agitation for social, political, and educational reform that immediately followed the protests came to be known as the May Fourth Movement.

In Changsha, Mao followed the burgeoning reform movement with keen interest. Inspired by the May Fourth Movement, he founded a newspaper, the *Xiang River Review,* to promote reform throughout China. At this point, Mao was not sure exactly what form his homeland's rehabilitation should take; he knew only that if China were to survive, its people must be prepared to embrace fundamental change. "We must all exert ourselves!" he admonished his readers. "We must all advance with the utmost strength! Our golden age, our age of glory and splendor, lies before us!"[7]

To use one of his own phrases, in 1919 Mao was still "looking for a road"—a creed on which to base his program for the political, economic, and social reformation of China.[8] In searching for his "road," Mao was drawn in turn to democratic reformism, anarchism, utopianism, and a host of other popular ideologies. By the following year, he was also developing a deep interest in another "ism"—socialism—a political and economic theory closely associated with the German thinker Karl Marx.

From a newly published Chinese translation of Marx's classic 1848 pamphlet, *The Communist Manifesto,* Mao learned that for "Marxist" socialists, class struggle is the driving force in history. According to Marxism, as nations became industrialized, the growing concentration of economic power in the capitalist class and their increasing oppression of the worker or proletariat class would ultimately lead to the overthrow of the capitalists by the proletariat. This proletariat revolution would be followed by the establishment of a classless "Communist" society in which private property would disappear and all resources and means of production such as farmland or factories that create a society's wealth would be held in common by the people. In a series of *New Youth* articles penned by Chen Duxiu, Mao also read with interest about the triumph of

In pursuing his education, Mao studied several ideologies —
including democratic reformism, anarchism, and utopianism — but
found his deepest interest in the ideas of Karl Marx (seen here),
author of the *Communist Manifesto*. Mao quickly saw the value
of Marxist socialism in addressing the problems that plagued
China and its people.

V. I. Lenin and his radical Bolsheviks in Russia following
the October Revolution of 1918, and the Bolsheviks' crusade
to transform their nation, now renamed the Soviet Union,
into a Communist state.

During 1920, Mao moved ever closer to embracing

Communism as his personal creed and the answer to his homeland's troubles. In this process, he was much influenced by his former boss at the Beijing University library, Li Dazhao, a recent convert to Communism, and another acquaintance from his Beijing days, Chen Duxiu, whose ardent belief in Communism, Mao later claimed, "deeply impressed me at what was probably a critical period of my life."[9] By the autumn of 1920, Mao had helped found a Marxist study circle in Changsha and a radical bookstore featuring Communist tracts. He also married Yang Kaihui, the daughter of his former teacher, Yang Changji.

By January 1921, Mao was at last ready to announce to his colleagues in the study circle and bookstore that he was a Communist. Mao was not alone: small Communist cells now existed in several Chinese cities, including Shanghai and Beijing. Since the spring of 1920, representatives from the Russian-led Comintern or Communist International had been laboring in China's urban areas to foster the development of a Chinese Communist movement. In July 1921, their efforts were rewarded when 13 Chinese delegates from the country's various Communist groups met secretly in Shanghai for the First Congress of the Chinese Communist Party (CCP). Among them was Mao Zedong, representing Changsha and Hunan. After years of searching, Mao had finally found a "road;" now he and his fellow Communist Party members had to convince the Chinese people to follow it.

3

Mao and the Young Chinese Communist Movement: 1921–1930

Shortly after the First Congress of the Chinese Communist Party (CCP) in July 1921, Mao helped found a branch of the new party in Hunan province. Two years later he was elected to the Central Committee of the CCP, the party's top council in organizational and political affairs.

During his first years with the CCP, Mao focused on building up the fledgling labor movement in Changsha. Since orthodox Marxists believe that Communist revolutions inevitably start with the urban proletariat, the CCP took as its first major task promoting workers' associations in China's cities. In late 1923, Mao's days as a labor organizer came to an abrupt end, however, when the local warlord banned all trade unions in Changsha.

After his attempts to organize laborers in Changsha were crushed by the local warlord, Mao committed himself to forging an alliance between the Chinese Communist Party and the more powerful Nationalist Party. In 1926, Mao persuaded the Nationalist Party to make him the principal of the Peasant Movement Training Institute in Canton.

THE UNITED FRONT AND THE NORTHERN EXPEDITION

With his labor activities in Changsha terminated, Mao threw himself into another project for his party—advancing the United Front, the new alliance between the CCP and the Nationalist Party (NP). The United Front had its roots in the Bolsheviks' commitment to promoting Communist revolution outside their homeland. Comintern representatives in China argued that in order to gain a foothold in the country, the CCP must ally itself with the larger and more powerful NP, which had recently established a shadow government in southern China. By pooling their resources, the two groups could defeat the regional warlords and imperialist foreigners wrecking havoc on China and reunite the nation. That crucial task accomplished, Lenin and his Comintern agents hoped that with the support of China's oppressed masses, the CCP would then wrest control of the country from the Nationalists. Sun no doubt surmised the Communists' ultimate ambitions in China but was confident that his more moderate party would prevail in the end. Hence, in 1923 he agreed to cooperate with the CCP in return for Soviet assistance in the form of money, weapons, and military advisers in his ongoing struggle against the warlords, the imperialists, and the tottering central government in Beijing.

During the mid-1920s, Mao became increasingly involved in the coalition with the Nationalists, even serving as head of the NP's propaganda department. In the wake of several large peasant demonstrations protesting foreign interference in China, he was also developing a deep interest in the revolutionary potential of the peasantry during this period. In 1926, Mao persuaded the NP leadership to make him principal of the recently established Peasant Movement Training Institute in Canton. The Institute's primary task was preparing rural organizers to mobilize China's peasantry for the planned United Front military campaign against the warlords and imperialist powers. Once the Institute was placed under Mao's direction, most of the young Chinese trained as rural organizers were CCP members, notes the historian Philip Short, a fact Mao did not make a point of advertising among the NP leadership.

That summer, an army under the command of Chiang Kaishek (the NP's new head following Sun Yatsen's death from cancer the previous year) set out from the party's southern headquarters to crush the powerful warlords of northern China once and for all. Chiang's Northern Expedition, as the military campaign was known, advanced rapidly through rural China, in part because of the assistance given his forces by mass movements in the countryside coordinated by organizers from Mao's Peasant Movement Training Institute.

In December 1926, Mao traveled to his home province of Hunan to observe for himself the popular movements sweeping the countryside with the launching of the Northern Expedition. These movements were not focused exclusively on aiding the Nationalist army in its military campaign, but rather had multiple goals, Mao noted. Among their central aims were reducing the exploitative land rents and interest rates the peasants had traditionally been compelled to pay to local landlords, replacing militias organized and commanded by landlords with peasant-led militias, and creating village assemblies through which peasants could play a role in running their local governments.

In a summary of his findings for the Central Committee written in early 1927, Mao stressed the revolutionary promise of China's downtrodden peasantry, arguing that if correctly handled by Communist organizers, the profound resentment of the peasants toward their landlord oppressors could be converted into revolutionary action. "In a very short period of time," he predicted, "several hundred million peasants in China's central, southern, and northern provinces will rise like a fierce wind or tempest, a force so swift and violent that no power, however great, will be able to suppress it. They will break through all the trammels that bind them and rush forward along the road to liberation."[10] Mao's impassioned account of Hunan's rebellious peasantry, however, made little impression on the CCP's top leadership, who clung resolutely to the traditional Marxist view of peasants as backward and unreliable and the urban proletariat as the fountainhead of Communist revolution.

FROM THE BARREL OF THE GUN

Just a few months after Mao wrote his optimistic report regarding the peasants' revolutionary possibilities, China's fledgling Communist movement received a devastating blow. In April 1927, Chiang Kaishek turned suddenly on his onetime allies, ordering the massacres of thousands of Communists in Shanghai and in cities and towns throughout southern China. With victory against the warlords and the weak Beijing regime now in sight for his army, Chiang decided that the time had come to crush the Communists, whose radical economic and political ideas alarmed him and many of his supporters among the propertied classes.

In a desperate bid to jump-start a revolution among the urban proletariat, the CCP tried to incite an uprising among the workers of Nanchang in August 1927. When that scheme fell through, despite their prejudices against the "backward" peasantry, frantic party leaders focused their attention on the countryside, planning a string of rural rebellions in China's southern provinces. Mao was ordered to lead a peasant insurrection in Hunan and then use the peasant rebels to capture the city of Changsha.

Mao's Autumn Harvest Uprising, as the new Communist offensive was known, was an unmitigated disaster. In the midst of a brutal Nationalist campaign of military repression, Mao proved unable to win more than a few followers from among the very same peasants whose revolutionary potential he had lauded in his report on the Hunan countryside just eight months earlier. Numbering less than 1,000 men, Mao's inexperienced little army was quickly crushed. Like the rest of China's Communist movement—including the Central Committee, which was reduced to directing

In 1927, with the warlords defeated and a weak government in Beijing, Nationalist Party leader Chiang Kaishek turned on his allies and ordered the massacre of Communists in Shanghai and other provinces. Mao's subsequent attempt to rouse the Chinese proletariat during the Autumn Harvest uprising was crushed with brutal efficiency.

party operations from a Shanghai hideaway—Mao and his ragtag army were forced underground. Eventually, they ended up in Jinggangshan, a mountainous no-man's-land about 130 miles from Changsha.

Mao detected a vital lesson in the dismaying events of the past few months: Chiang's bloody purge, the abject failures of the Nanchang and Autumn Harvest rebellions, the humiliating flight to Jinggangshan. Chiang and his Nationalist Party, Mao noted, "rose by grasping the gun."[11] The time was long overdue for the CCP to follow their example: "From now on, we should pay the greatest attention to military affairs. We must know that political power is obtained from the barrel of the gun."[12] If the Communists had any hope of achieving their revolutionary goals, Mao insisted, they first needed to build a well-trained army.

Mao's idea held little appeal for the CCP leadership, which had always looked on the oppressed urban masses, not a professional army, as the principal motor of the revolution. A Communist victory in China, the CCP leaders maintained, would be rooted in popular indignation and spontaneous violence, not in systematic military force, as Mao suggested.

For Mao, however, the party leadership in far-off Shanghai might as well have been on another planet. Free to follow his own course in his isolated mountain hideout, Mao was soon aided in his crusade to build a more effective fighting force by the arrival of several other fleeing

Mao: A Life

In 1926, as mass movements inspired by the Northern Expedition swept across China's countryside, many peasants took advantage of the chaos to seek revenge against exploitative landlords, publicly humiliating and beating them (and in some cases, killing them). Early in 1927, Mao defended the peasants' "unruly" behavior before the CCP's Central Committee in what would be his first public espousal of mass violence as an appropriate means of achieving political ends:

> True, the peasants are in a sense "unruly" in the countryside. . . .
> They have even created a kind of terror in the countryside. This
> is what ordinary people call "going too far," or "going beyond
> the proper limits in righting a wrong" . . . Such talk may seen
> plausible, but in fact it is wrong. . . . A revolution is not like
> inviting people to dinner, or writing an essay, or painting a picture,
> or doing embroidery, it cannot be so refined, so leisurely and
> gentle. . . . A revolution . . . is an act of violence whereby one
> class overthrows the power of another. . . . If the peasants do not
> use extremely great force, they cannot possibly overthrow the
> deeply rooted power of the landlords. . . . (Mao, quoted in Philip
> Short, *Mao*, p. 172–73).

Communist armies, the largest one led by an experienced officer named Zhu De. Merging forces, Mao and Zhu created the Fourth Red Army—or the Mao-Zhu Army, as it was popularly known. (According to Communist tradition, the use of the name "Red Army" for the Communist forces goes back to the abortive Nanchang uprising of August 1927; red is the color of international communism.) Determined to transform the undisciplined peasants under his command into a force capable of resisting Chiang's far larger and better-equipped army, Mao devoted much of his time at Jinggangshan to reading and thinking about military issues.

FASHIONING A REVOLUTIONARY ARMY

During the winter of 1929, Mao decided to move from Jinggangshan to a new base in southern Jiangxi on the border of Fujian province, where the climate was milder and the terrain less rugged. The Jiangxi Soviet, as the new base came to be known, would be Mao's home for the next five years. In Jiangxi, Mao put into practice several critical principles he had formulated during his earlier sojourn at Jinggangshan.

First, Mao insisted that to become a more effective and cohesive fighting force, the Red Army must be politicized. A thorough political indoctrination would reinforce the soldiers' sense of solidarity as well as their will to fight, even against vastly superior forces, by helping them to understand exactly what it was they were being asked to risk their lives for. Every Red Army member must be given a "political education" in order to become "class-conscious."[13] Once the peasant soldiers truly understood the evils of the current class system and the benefits that the more equitable economic and social system advocated by the Communists would bring to themselves and their families, they would "know they are fighting for themselves," Mao reasoned, and "hence they can endure the hardships of the bitter struggle without complaint."[14] To facilitate the soldiers' political indoctrination, each man was assigned to a small squad led by a Communist Party member.

Second, to help the soldiers better comprehend the social and economic ideals stressed in the army's indoctrination program and to increase morale among the rank and file, Mao fashioned a more egalitarian military force at Jiangxi than had ever existed in China. In Mao's "military democracy" there was no saluting, no special uniform for officers, and no insignia of rank.[15] Soldiers addressed officers by attaching the term "comrade" to their specific job titles, for example, "comrade platoon leader" or "comrade company commander."[16] Everyone received the same pay and ate the same food. Battle plans were to be reviewed with the entire army ahead of time so that each man could understand his part in the proposed military action and why it was important to the success of the mission as a whole.

The last significant principle Mao strove to put into practice in his Jiangxi base was that the army must make every effort to win over the peasant masses. The Communist victory, Mao believed, depended on the people's backing, for the peasants were the "sea" in which the Red Army "fish" must swim.[17] He was convinced that the Communist movement could endure during this period of intense persecution only by establishing a series of rural bases such as his own in southern Jiangxi and relying on the surrounding peasant population for food and other critical supplies, transport, recruits, and intelligence reports. Ultimately, Mao contended, "the richest source of power to wage war lies in the masses of the people."[18]

For Mao, the creation and strict enforcement of a comprehensive code of moral behavior for his soldiers was a key means of gaining the people's loyalty and assistance. In common with the armies of China's imperial era, the Nationalist and warlord armies all too often treated the peasantry with contempt—looting or destroying their homes, livestock, and crops, and on occasion, even raping, beating, or murdering them. In contrast, Mao sought to create a sense of unity and sympathy between the Communist forces and the masses by presenting his troops as the protectors and advocates of the common people. The warriors of the young Red Army would disprove the old Chinese saying that you do not use high-quality iron to make nails or virtuous men to make soldiers.

To ensure that his troops consistently treated civilians with decency and respect, Mao issued a set of ethical guidelines known as the "Eight Points of Behavior." Soldiers were commanded to replenish straw bedding after being quartered in a peasant's home, give back anything they borrowed from civilians, reimburse them promptly for any damaged items, never strike at civilians, be honest in all business transactions, be polite, refrain from taking sexual liberties with women, and act humanely toward prisoners. Added to these eight points were the "Three Rules for Behavior": Always obey orders, do not steal so much as a single needle or thread from the people, and promptly turn in everything captured from the enemy. Under the new guidelines, a soldier caught committing a serious offense against civilians such as rape, murder, or robbery was to be shot on the spot.

Mao's more virtuous and egalitarian army garnered the Communists many loyal supporters in southern Jiangxi, with one consequence being a steady influx of new peasant recruits for the Mao-Zhou Army. The peasants were also won over to the Communist side in large numbers by the land reform program Mao instituted near his Jiangxi base. Under Mao's program, farmland was confiscated from landlords and redistributed to the poor peasants who actually tilled the fields. Mao's Soviet was not China's sole Communist base—several other bases had also been established in out-of-the-way spots in southern China after Chiang Kaishek's violent purge of 1927. Yet by 1930, the Jiangxi Soviet had emerged as the largest and strongest center of Communist influence in the entire country, encompassing much of the southern portion of the province and occupying a region a little larger than the country of Belgium.

A DISASTROUS CAMPAIGN

The CCP leadership in Shanghai was heartened by reports of Mao's success in Jiangxi and by the steadily expanding forces of the other, smaller Communist bases scattered throughout southern China. Indeed, the CCP officials were so impressed that by mid-1930, they had decided the time was ripe for the Communists to take another shot at capturing China's major cities. As in the summer of 1927, their goal in targeting cities was to incite a full-scale rebellion by the urban proletariat against the country's exploitative economic system and the political leaders who upheld that system.

Mao, who had far more faith in the revolutionary potential of China's 250 million rural peasants than its 1.5 million industrial workers, could muster little enthusiasm for the Central Committee's renewed campaign to provoke revolution among the urban proletariat. Only reluctantly did he order his Red Army unit to attack Changsha, the largest nearby city. Although Mao's troops held Changsha briefly, they and the other Communist units based in southern China proved no match for the superior Nationalist forces. Moreover, as in the abortive Nanchang rebellion of 1927, the nationwide workers' revolt that was supposed to follow the Red Army's attacks never materialized. Consequently, when the CCP leadership ordered a second assault on Changsha, Mao refused to comply, retreating with his men to their base in southern Jiangxi. Meanwhile, back in Changsha where Yang Kaihui and her three small sons by Mao had been living since his flight to Jinggangshan, local authorities beheaded Mao's wife as a reprisal for the Red's earlier attack on the city.

The CCP's campaign to incite rebellion in China's urban centers had been an unqualified failure. Nonetheless, it made a deep impression on Chiang Kaishek, who had successfully completed his Northern Expedition in 1928 and now governed the country from his capital at Nanjing on the Yangtze River. Determined to crush the troublesome Communists once and for all, Chiang began planning a military offensive against their southern bases, and particularly against the largest and strongest of them all, Mao's Jiangxi Soviet.

4

The Encirclement Campaigns and the Long March: 1930–1935

Late in the summer of 1930, Chiang Kaishek announced that he was assembling a force of 100,000 men that would smash China's "Red menace" before the year was out.[19] Confident that Mao and Zhu De's 40,000 peasant troops could easily be routed, Chiang turned his anti-Red campaign over to the forces of local warlords with whom he had made alliances instead of using the central government's more professional and better- equipped army. Chiang, however, had underestimated the discipline and motivation of the Red troops who had been so meticulously trained and indoctrinated at the Jiangxi base. He had also miscalculated the resourcefulness of their leader Mao Zedong, particularly his genius for guerrilla warfare.

By 1930, Chiang Kaishek (shown here) recognized the growing threat of Mao's Red Army and was committed to its destruction. Chiang, however, grossly underestimated the discipline and motivation of Mao's troops, as well as the resourcefulness of their leader.

MAO'S GUERRILLA STRATEGY

In December 1930, Chiang launched his first encirclement campaign or "bandit suppression drive," as he liked to call the anti-Communist offensive.[20] Keenly aware that his forces lacked both the manpower and firepower to prevail over the Nationalists in a conventional conflict, Mao believed that the Reds' primary goal should not be to hold onto territory. Instead, their central aim should be to chip away at the enemy's superior strength while preserving as many of their own forces as possible. Unless absolutely confident of victory, therefore, Mao avoided positional warfare in favor of a hit-and-run guerrilla strategy, which he summarized for his men in a few easy-to-remember verses:

> [When the] enemy advances, we withdraw,
> [When the] enemy rests, we harass,
> [When the] enemy tires, we attack,
> [When the] enemy withdraws, we pursue.[21]

Although far more numerous than the Red Army, the warlord troops were not as ably commanded. Consequently, they entered the Red base areas in a number of spread-out columns. The Nationalists' flawed tactics played right into Mao's hands. In keeping with his guerrilla-based strategy, he lured the dispersed units deeper and deeper into the rugged terrain of the Soviet. For weeks, Chiang's forces pursued the elusive Reds as they retreated swiftly across the craggy base area without once giving battle. When the Nationalist army lines were stretched thin, Mao suddenly made his move, consolidating his forces for lightning-fast assaults on his foe's well-separated and by now thoroughly exhausted units. As soon as the enemy troops had been routed, the Reds quickly dispersed before other nearby Nationalist units could arrive on the scene. "Lightly equipped and thoroughly familiar with the terrain of their base area, the Communists could move far more rapidly than their opponents," notes the military historian John Elting.[22]

By late January 1931, Chiang's first encirclement campaign had ended in humiliating defeat and Mao's attacks on isolated Nationalist divisions had garnered the Reds a fine arsenal of rifles, other weapons, and some 12,000 prisoners. Many of the captured men, impressed by the Communists' more egalitarian and competently managed army, willingly joined Mao's forces when offered the opportunity. Mao's pragmatic strategy of luring the Nationalist forces deep into

Communist-held territory and then routing detached units had proved a brilliant success.

Chiang, however, was not about to give up so quickly. In April, he launched his second encirclement campaign against the Jiangxi base. This time, Chiang doubled the number of his warlord forces. He was confident that his 200,000 troops would make short work of the Communists. The Nationalists' additional manpower, however, proved of little help against the determined Reds and their wily leader. Repeating the same mistake they had made in the first campaign, the Nationalists allowed themselves to be

Sun Tzu and *The Art of War*

During the years he spent in Jinggangshan and the Jiangxi Soviet, Mao devoted much time to studying the writings of China's traditional military thinkers—particularly the country's most famous military strategist, the fifth-century B.C. general, Sun Tzu. In his celebrated book, *The Art of War*, Sun Tzu taught that it is not the quantity or the type of equipment that counts in war, nor is it the number of soldiers; rather it is how the commander chooses to use them. High morale among the ranks and a well-thought-out strategy were far more important than superior numbers or weapons, Sun asserted. Mao was drawn to many of Sun's military principles, including his admonition to "avoid what is strong to strike what is weak," and his emphasis on the value of deception in warfare. Regarding the development of a strategy based on deception, Sun advised his readers:

Hence, when able to attack we must seem unable; when using our forces, we must seem inactive; when we are near, we must make the enemy believe that we are far away; when far away, we must make him believe we are near. Hold out baits to entice the enemy. Feign disorder, and crush him. . . . Pretend to be weak, that he may grow arrogant. . . . Attack him where unprepared, where you are not expected (Sun Tzu, quoted in John R. Elting, *The Superstrategists*, p. 224–25).

lured deep into Red territory, marching their troops into the rugged, Communist-held areas in seven widely separated columns. By concentrating his forces against one enemy column at a time in whirlwind attacks, Mao was again able to demolish the Nationalists' offensive power, even though their combined forces outnumbered his own by more than five to one. By the end of May, the second "bandit suppression drive" had ended with another ignominious defeat for Chiang.

For his third campaign against the Communists in the summer of 1931, a deeply frustrated Chiang took personal charge, assembling a force of 300,000 — including 100,000 well-equipped government troops. This time, Chiang's commanders made sure that none of their divisions became isolated, and although 30,000 Nationalist troops were killed, taken prisoner, or wounded in the fighting, the Nationalists also managed to inflict heavy losses on the Reds, in marked contrast with their two previous campaigns.

In early September, however, the Communists' fortunes took a dramatic turn for the better when several of Chiang's warlord rivals formed an alliance and marched troops into Hunan province in an audacious attempt to bring southern China under their rule. Chiang quickly abandoned Jiangxi to stamp out this new and unexpected threat to his power. Later that same month, the armies of imperial Japan invaded the vast, mineral-rich region of Manchuria in northeastern China, providing another major distraction for Chiang from his anti-Communist offensive. It would be a full year before Chiang refocused his attention on China's "Red menace."

MAO FINDS HIMSELF SIDELINED

Although Mao had been given a much-needed respite in his struggle against the forces of Chiang Kaishek, he was facing other grave battles within his own party in the autumn of

1931. For the past year, the "Twenty-Eight Bolsheviks," a group of young Chinese men educated in the Soviet Union, had dominated the Central Committee. From their underground headquarters in Shanghai, the Bolshevik faction and their leader, Bo Gu, denounced Mao's guerrilla strategy in Jiangxi as ill-conceived and overly cautious, in spite of Mao's impressive record in the encirclement campaigns. Determined to follow the tactics used by the Bolsheviks in crushing their opponents following the Revolution of 1917 and grossly overestimating the Red Army's strength, the CCP's new ruling clique favored conventional open warfare and capturing major cities over what they derided as Mao's rural "guerrillaism."[23] Mao, they accused, had timidly clung to a "pure defense line" in Jiangxi of "luring the enemy in deep" and "waiting by a tree-stump for the rabbits to dash up and throw themselves against it."[24]

There was only so much Bo Gu and the rest of the Twenty-Eight Bolsheviks could do about Mao's military methods from their hideout in distant Shanghai. By early 1932, however, all that changed when most of the faction, along with the French-educated Zhou Enlai, arrived in Jiangxi in the wake of an intensified police campaign to flush out CCP members from China's cities. Soon, Mao found himself being sidelined by the new refugees in the base he had labored so hard to build up and defend. Although Mao was awarded with the title of Chairman of the Chinese Soviet Republic (as the Jiangxi Soviet was now called) in late 1931, his impressive-sounding new post was in fact largely honorific, with most of the actual military and political power in Jiangxi being held by Bo Gu and Zhou Enlai.

In January 1933, Japanese troops still occupied Manchuria, yet Chiang was anxious to crush his Communist rivals. Although his forces shattered another smaller Communist base in southern China, Chiang still could not bring down the central Red base at Jiangxi. Quietly abandoning the "forward and offensive line" they had earlier endorsed as the new Communist military policy, by April 1933 Bo Gu and Zhou Enlai had managed to rout Chiang's fourth encirclement campaign using hit-and-run tactics that owed much to Mao's "guerrillaism."[25] Bo Gu and Zhou Enlai were also significantly aided in their victory by widespread public dissatisfaction with Chiang for attacking the Reds instead of going after Manchuria's foreign invaders. In an effort to placate his disgruntled compatriots, in March Chiang had sent one-third of the 150,000 troops in the Jiangxi campaign on the long trek north toward Manchuria.

Chiang's removal of 50,000 troops from Mao's base area in the spring of 1933 to northern China turned out to be a phony gesture, however. In fact, the troops were never used against Manchuria's Japanese occupiers, and by that autumn Nationalist armies were once again descending on the Chinese Soviet Republic as well as on smaller Communist bases elsewhere in southern China. Determined to vanquish his domestic opponents before making war against the Japanese, Chiang proclaimed defiantly, "the Japanese are a disease of the skin. The Communists are a disease of the heart."[26]

With the assistance of German military advisors, Chiang devised a new strategy for what he hoped would be his final campaign against the Communists. After encircling the Jiangxi base areas with barbed wire, trenches, and 14,000 stone blockhouses to strangle any Red troop movement, Chiang herded the CCP's peasant supporters into concentration camps well away from the forces they had spied for and supplied with food and other necessities.

Although their forces were vastly outgunned and outnumbered by the 800,000-strong Nationalist army, at a January 1934 meeting of the Central Committee, the CCP leadership strongly advocated a military policy of direct frontal assaults. In adopting this bold—and unrealistic— plan, they were greatly influenced by a recent arrival at the Jiangxi base, the Comintern representative Otto Braun. In the few short months since he had come to the base, Braun, who had spent three years at a Moscow military academy studying conventional warfare and fancied himself a great military expert, had gained considerable sway over both Bo Gu and Zhou Enlai. According to Braun, the era of defensive guerrilla warfare had ended for the Communists, and a new age of fighting positional or regular warfare had begun. He admonished the Reds to defend every inch of their territory.

But as the Nationalists tightened their noose around the Jiangxi base and the Communists began running out of essential supplies, even the hawkish Braun realized that the Reds had little choice but to make a run for it. Thus, on the night of October 15, 1934, some 72,000 Red soldiers and 15,000 other Communists set off on what came to be known as the Long March, a 370-day endurance test in which the marchers hiked 6,000 miles, traversing barren plateaus, fetid swamplands, 24 major rivers, and 18 mountain ranges along their way. Destined to become an emblem of the Communists' courage, stamina, and unswerving devotion to their cause, the Long March was, in reality, an act of desperation, a last-ditch effort to save the CCP and the Red Army from complete annihilation at the hands of Chiang's forces.

THE LONG MARCH

Mao and his second wife, He Zizhen, a young peasant woman whom he had married soon after receiving news of Yang Kaihui's execution, were among the perhaps 87,000 Communists who fled the Jiangxi base in mid-October

With renewed aggression, Nationalist forces again attempted to wipe out the Red Army in 1934. Seeing no other way to avoid certain death and the destruction of the Red Army, Mao's followers set out on the "Long March"—a 6,000-mile (9,660-kilometer) trek across harsh terrain—with the Nationalist forces in pursuit.

1934. Not accompanying Mao and He Zizhen was their two-year-old son, who had been left in the care of a local peasant family. He Zizhen was one of a handful of women—most of them wives or mistresses of CCP officials—who participated in the Long March.

Although the marchers lacked a clearly formulated plan, a majority of the CCP leadership favored hiking northwest toward a small Communist base in Hunan province some 400 miles away. There, they would build a new central Communist base area to take the place of the one they were abandoning in Jiangxi. Before beginning their long trek, however, the marchers' first task was to break out of the Jiangxi base area, which was surrounded by four well-entrenched lines of Chiang's forces. By moving out under the cover of darkness and along remote trails known only to the Reds, the marchers were able to slip through the web of blockhouses and trenches with surprising ease. Indeed, it was three weeks before the Nationalists even comprehended that their quarry had escaped.

In late November, the refugees reached the Xiang River, which they had to cross to get to the Communist base in Hunan. By this time, however, Chiang's aircraft and information network had managed to discover their exact location in northern Guangxi province. In a devastating week-long battle with much larger and better-armed Nationalist forces, the Communists lost over half of their army. At last, the battered Communist band managed to cross the river into southern Hunan and duck their pursuers.

The marchers were now confronted with the dilemma of where to go next. Although 300,000 Nationalist troops blocked the route northward to the Communist base in Hunan, Otto Braun and Bo Gu demanded that the refugees stick with their original plan. Mao, however, had another idea—give up on Hunan and head westward into the steep mountains of Guizhou province where the Nationalists were weak.

It was Mao's proposal, not Braun and Bo Gu's plan, that won the support of the majority of the CCP and Red Army officials. Undoubtedly, this was due in no small measure to Mao's telling criticisms of the two leaders' tactics during the Xiang River calamity. Braun and Bo Gu bore direct responsibility for the costly debacle, Mao argued: Instead of using the tactic of feint to confuse the Nationalists after the marchers broke out of the Jiangxi base area, they had led the Communists along a predictable straight-line route to the river. Moreover, casualties would have been much lower during the crossing if the columns had been able to move more quickly, Mao contended. Instead, they were slowed down by the heavy loads of office equipment, furniture, and CCP documents that Bo and Braun had insisted on bringing along.

A few weeks after the devastating battle at Xiang River, the marchers reached the city of Zunyi in northwestern Guizhou province. There the CCP officials held a conference to consider future plans. Mao took the opportunity to once more blast Braun and Bo Gu's uninspired leadership of the March. Their unwillingness to employ a strategy of deception and feint, along with blind faith in the superiority of conventional warfare, spelled disaster for the Reds, he argued. The Communists, he declared, must return to "the basic strategic and tactical principles with which the Red Army [had in the past] won victories," i.e., the "flexible guerrilla strategy" which Mao and Zhu De had used so effectively in Jiangxi during Chiang's early encirclement campaigns.[27] The Reds had to change their military line immediately, he warned. The very survival of the CCP was at stake.

By the second day of the conference, Mao had won a powerful and highly articulate ally for his cause—Zhou Enlai. When Zhou suggested that Mao assume leadership over the March, most party officials quickly followed his lead. By the end of the meeting, Mao had persuaded his colleagues to endorse a series of resolutions "that read like a summation of all his favorite military ideas," according to the historian Ross Terrill.[28] Most significantly, the conferees resolved that since the Communist army was far smaller and less well-equipped than its pursuers, the Reds must concentrate their forces on points of Nationalist weakness, attacking isolated enemy units and avoiding Chiang's main forces at all costs.

In addition to formulating a new military line for the marchers at Zunyi, Mao also provided them with an official purpose: to march northward and fight the Japanese armies who were steadily expanding beyond Manchuria into other areas of northern China. No longer was the Long March a "ragged military retreat," writes Terrill.[29] For now, the marchers were not merely running away from Chiang's forces; they were heading off to do battle with the Japanese, who must be expelled before the nation could be reunited under any government—Communist or otherwise. As Mao later told the American journalist Edgar Snow: "We cannot even discuss communism if we are robbed of a country in which to practice it."[30] According to Mao's inspiring new vision for the Long March, the participants were on a noble and patriotic crusade, a mission possessing "a national as well as a revolutionary purpose."[31]

MAO LEADS THE COMMUNISTS TO SAFETY

Mao left Zunyi in late January 1935 with perhaps 5,000 civilians and approximately 30,000 troops, thousands of whom were either peasant volunteers or Red soldiers from other beleaguered Communist bases in southern China who had joined the march along the way. To get north, the Communists needed to first cross the vast Yangtze River. Mao soon discovered, however, that Chiang had stationed troops at every possible crossing. During the next six weeks, Mao, with the assistance of his top general, Zhu De, managed to completely confuse the Nationalists regarding the Reds' location and intentions. He instituted a series of feints, including sudden shifts in direction, night marches, and whirlwind assaults on isolated Nationalist units in what the military historian Bevin Alexander calls "a campaign almost unparalleled in deception, speed of movement, and unexpected descent upon the enemy forces."[32]

After a humiliated Chiang moved a large number of new troops into the Zunyi area, however, Mao decided that he could shake off his pursuer only by marching further south into Guizhou, then veering west through rugged Yunnan province, and finally north again to the upper reaches of the Yangtze. On arriving at the Upper Yangtze, Mao ordered his vanguard to create a diversion while the main army captured the ferry crossing and successfully crossed north into Sichuan province.

Incensed that the Communists had outwitted him again, Chiang mobilized his troops to intercept the Reds at another river about 200 miles north of where they had traversed the Upper Yangtze, the Dadu. But Mao's little army would not be stopped. After Nationalist troops began bombing the ferry crossing that the Red vanguard had just used to traverse the Dadu, Mao ordered his main force to race nearly 100 miles upstream to the village of Luding, where an ancient suspension bridge spanned the raging river. Fashioned from 13 iron chains upon which boards had been laid for flooring, the narrow bridge swayed a dizzying 370 feet above the Dadu's deep, swirling waters.

When they arrived at the Luding crossing, the Reds discovered that Nationalist soldiers stationed in a gatehouse on the other side of the river had removed two-thirds of the flooring from the 360-foot-long bridge and were preparing to set fire to the remaining planks at their end. What followed next was destined to become one of the most famous incidents in Chinese Communist history. With rifles and hand grenades strapped to their backs, 22 intrepid Red soldiers inched across the bare chains under heavy machine-gun fire from the Nationalist defenders, then battled their way through the flames engulfing the final third of the bridge. Against all odds, 18 of the 22 men completed the crossing. Within two hours, Chiang's garrison had been routed and both the bridge and the town of Luding were under Communist control.

Still, the marchers' long ordeal was not over. During the summer and early autumn of 1935, they endured what turned out to be the deadliest interval of their entire trek as they struggled through the vast swamplands and rugged, snowbound mountains that lay between the Dadu River and remote Shaanxi province, where they now hoped to establish their new northern base. During this final leg of their journey, thousands of the marchers died from disease (brought on by frigid temperatures and constant damp) hunger, and dehydration.

In October 1935, Mao and his weary, battered group finally reached the village of Wayabao in northern Shaanxi, where a small band of Communist refugees had already formed a base. Perhaps 6,000 of the approximately 87,000 marchers who set out with him from Jiangxi had managed to finish the perilous, yearlong odyssey.

Most historians stress Mao's crucial role in shepherding China's Communist remnant to safety in their new refuge in northern Shaanxi. Mao's "drive and skill," writes Terrill, were "an indispensable ingredient in the success of the Long March."[33] Yet it was not only Mao's military ingenuity or unwavering determination that made the March a success, he points out. Mao showed true political genius in his leadership of the March, Terrill contends, when he developed an inspiring new goal for the marchers and for the CCP itself at the Zunyi Conference—to go north and fight the Japanese. Mao's vision for the struggling Communist movement "filled the vacuum of the CCP's *raison d'etre* after the miserable collapse of the Jiangxi base," writes Terrill. Moreover, he asserts, "it unlocked the Communists from a cage of sectarianism, and made them patriots in the eyes of millions of Chinese who did not know Marx from the moon."[34]

Despite their lack of a clear plan, the Communist marchers managed to escape the Nationalist troops after a bitter fight at the Xiang River. It was not until October 1935—after suffering through swampland, disease, hunger, and frigid temperatures— that the remains of the Red Army reached a Communist refugee camp and safety.

Millions of ordinary Chinese were indeed touched by the Long March. For in the course of their 370-day trek, the Communists were thrust into close contact with Chinese peasants from nearly a dozen provinces. Determined to make as much of the opportunity as possible, they planted the seeds of Communist revolution wherever they went, explaining their political and social ideals through dance, song, drama, and other techniques designed to appeal to their generally illiterate audiences. As they spread their Communist message among the masses, the marchers also took pains to stress their deep commitment to saving China from its Japanese invaders. They hardly needed to point out that theirs' was a commitment Chiang Kaishek failed to share, since he chose to use the Nationalist Army to hound his Communist compatriots rather than the Japanese intruders.

As the historian Shaun Breslin writes, Mao and the other marchers ably "used the Nationalists' own apparent failings in defending China's national sovereignty to push their own nationalist credentials" among their compatriots.[35] Mao understood well the immense propaganda value of the Long March: It "has proclaimed to the world that the Red Army is an army of heroes," he declared; "it has announced to some 200 million people in 11 provinces that the road of the Red Army is their only road to liberation."[36]

In Shaanxi, with their Long March finally complete, Mao and his Communist colleagues set about the task of mapping a future course for their movement. As it turned out, pressing military challenges would engage most of the Communists' attention and energy over the next decade, as Mao led them in battle first against the armies of imperial Japan, and then in a final showdown against the forces of their old enemy, Chiang Kaishek.

5

Fighting the Japanese and the Nationalists: 1936–1949

Mao soon discovered that northern Shaanxi was not the safe haven for the Communists he had hoped it would be. Warlord armies aligned with Chiang Kaishek surrounded the new base on three sides. Of these various forces, Mao judged the large North-East Army led by the Manchurian warlord Zhang Xueliang to be the most fragile link in the Nationalist coalition. Aware that Manchuria's Japanese occupiers had murdered Zhang's father, Mao presumed that Zhang would be eager to avenge his parent's death and drive the invaders from his homeland. Hence, Mao flooded Zhang's headquarters with requests for a cease-fire and a unified campaign against their mutual Japanese enemy. "We are Chinese," Mao wrote. "We

Mao, seen here in 1936 wearing a Communist-style hat, won the loyalty of many of China's people. It was this popular allegiance that ultimately helped Mao defeat Chiang Kaishek.

live in the same land. The Red Army and the North-East Army are from the same Chinese earth. Why should we be enemies? Why should we kill each other?"[37]

THE SECOND UNITED FRONT AND WAR WITH JAPAN

By late 1936, Zhang had been completely won over by Mao's nationalist arguments. When Chiang Kaishek flew to Shaanxi's capital city of Xian to coordinate what he hoped would be his final campaign against the Communists in their new base in December, instead of cooperating with Chiang as he had earlier pledged to do, Zhang kidnapped the NP leader. Maintaining that the Japanese constituted a far greater threat to China than the Communists, the Manchurian warlord refused to release Chiang until he agreed to stop persecuting the Reds and focused instead on fighting the country's imperialist invaders from the East. To assure victory over the Japanese, Zhang further insisted, Chiang must commit himself to forming a united front composed of all patriotic Chinese groups, including the Reds.

Chiang had little choice but to agree to his captors' demands, although like Mao, he assumed that the United Front would last only as long as the war with Japan and had no plans for sharing the postwar future with his rivals. By the summer of 1937, the specific provisions of the Second United Front between the NP and the CCP had been all but worked out—and just in time. On July 7, Japanese troops performing military exercises near Beijing accused Chinese troops of firing on them, providing the Japanese government with an excuse to launch a full-scale invasion of China. The Sino-Japanese War had begun.

The Japanese campaign first centered on Shanghai, where Nationalist defenders suffered heavy losses, then moved to Chiang's capital city of Nanjing, where hundreds of thousands of Chinese civilians, including many women and children, were slaughtered by Japanese troops in December 1937. In the meantime, Chiang and the Nationalist government retreated from the massive Japanese offensive to Chongqing in Sichuan province in the remote southwest of China.

By 1939, Japanese forces controlled much of northern China, along with strategic seaports and industrial cities farther south. As the now-united Chinese forces waged war against the Japanese, Mao began to write down the lessons he had learned in his military campaigns. His essays "Problems of Strategy in Guerrilla War" and "On Protracted War" would prove influential in guiding future Red Army tactics.

By 1939, Japanese forces controlled much of north China and the major industrial cities and seaports in southeast and south-central China. In Sichuan, Chiang found himself isolated from the areas that had traditionally comprised his chief source of revenue and support. While Chiang was holed up in remote Chongqing, however, Mao and his fellow Communists were actually extending their influence and power within their beleaguered homeland.

From the Communists' central base area—the town of Yanan in northern Shaanxi—Red soldiers and CCP cadres (party professionals) spread out through rural central and northern China, using guerrilla warfare to establish and defend numerous base areas behind the Japanese lines. By 1940, as many as 50 million Chinese lived within these Red base areas. Thousands were refugees fleeing the Japanese armies, but most were local residents who provided critical support to the Red Army in the form of recruits, intelligence work, transport, food, and other necessities.

Indeed, the Communists were remarkably successful in winning broad popular support in the rural areas they penetrated. Their outspoken commitment to ousting the Japanese invaders appealed to the nationalistic feelings of their compatriots, and the guerrilla campaigns they waged against the Japanese behind enemy lines won them a great deal of favorable publicity. Despite their popularity among the masses, however, it is impossible to say whether the Reds' sporadic assaults on isolated enemy forces "really troubled the Japanese appreciably," writes John Elting.[38]

In gaining the backing of the rural masses, most historians agree, the Communists' economic reform program was as important as their nationalistic fervor. Everywhere the Reds established bases, Mao ordered that land rents and interest rates paid by poorer peasants be reduced. To avoid antagonizing the rural upper and middle classes, however, he eschewed the more radical policy implemented in the Jiangxi Soviet of confiscating land from landlords and redistributing it to the peasants.

MAO IN YANAN

As Red soldiers and cadres fanned out from Yanan into the Chinese countryside during the early years of the Sino-Japanese War, Mao remained at the CCP headquarters, where he devoted much of his time to writing about political and military issues. During this period, he produced a number of classic essays on military topics, including two that would prove particularly influential in guiding Red Army tactics and strategy during the decade ahead: "Problems of Strategy in Guerrilla War" and "On Protracted War."

In "Problems of Strategy in Guerrilla War," Mao summarized many of the military principles he had relied on since his Jiangxi days. He advised establishing bases in rural areas, drawing the enemy deep into the base territory, and then using mobile guerrilla warfare to wear him down and chip away at his superior forces. The weaker force in a conflict must excel in mobile warfare, Mao stressed, meaning "to fight when you can win, move away when you can't win."[39] To preserve troop strength, the inferior opponent must always be prepared to retreat quickly. Yet, as the historian Shu Guang Zhang explains, Mao also believed that mobile warfare "should be employed not merely to avoid setbacks but also to create opportunities for retaliation when victory was more certain."[40] Retreat could allow a commander to more effectively concentrate his forces against dispersed enemy forces, to employ "several divisions against one enemy division, . . . several columns against one [enemy] column," Mao asserted.[41]

In "On Protracted War," Mao focused on the dilemma of how China's army could rout the more modernized military of imperial Japan. According to Mao, a protracted (drawn-out) war strategy could mean the difference between victory and defeat for the Second United Front in their campaign against Japan, or for any belligerent forced to combat a superior army. Waging an extended war would permit the underdog to progressively build up its own forces while gradually depleting the enemy's strength and morale. This would eventually enable the inferior force to switch from a largely defensive guerrilla strategy to an offensive strategy utilizing large armies in stand-up fights. Realizing that the Reds would almost certainly find themselves at war again with the Nationalists in the future, Mao probably had Chiang in mind as much as the Japanese when he wrote, "The enemy wants to fight a short war, but we just will not do it. The enemy has internal conflicts. He just wants to defeat us and then to return to his own internal battles. . . . We will let him stew, and then, when his own internal problems become acute, we will smite him a mighty blow." [42]

Mao emphasized the critical importance of attaining mass support for the armed forces, a principle he had embraced since his days in Jiangxi, in "On Protracted War" and his other military essays of the Yanan period. All Chinese must be drawn into the army's crusade against the enemy — young and old, male and female alike. To gain the masses' loyalty and assistance, Mao argued, the people must be politically informed, for even "a national revolutionary war . . . cannot be won without . . . telling the . . . people about the political aim of the war. It is necessary for every soldier and civilian to understand why the war must be fought and how it concerns him." [43]

While Mao was writing prolifically on military and political issues in Yanan, he was also working to consolidate his position as supreme leader of the CCP, a position he had held informally since the Zunyi Conference. To weed out his rivals and opponents within the Party and elevate himself to a position of undisputed authority, in 1942 Mao launched a "Rectification Campaign" in which party members were compelled to study Mao's writings as the essential statement of what he referred to as the "sinification" of Marxism. For Mao, sinifying Marxism meant adopting Marx's economic and political theories to specific Chinese conditions. In such essays as the famous "On Practice," Mao emphasized that unlike either Marx's Germany or Lenin's Russia, China lacked a sizable urban proletariat. Therefore, he asserted, China's revolution must be rooted in the country's vast and disgruntled peasantry, and not in the industrial workers identified by Marx and Lenin as the core of Communist revolution. Any Chinese Communist who failed to understand the need to harmonize Communist theory with Chinese realities, he proclaimed, was guilty of "serious errors," errors that the entire party must work together to "resolutely overcome."[44]

Perhaps it was inevitable that as Mao's political texts became compulsory reading for Chinese Communists and rival political lines were formally denounced, the Rectification Campaign would degenerate into a brutal purge of CCP members deemed insufficiently devoted to "Mao Zedong Thought," as the leader's sinified Marxism was now called. Perhaps it was also inevitable that as Mao Zedong Thought was transformed into party dogma, a full-blown personality cult of Mao would take root in China, with gigantic portraits of the leader painted on town walls and government buildings in Red areas. The new Maoist cult even gained its own anthem during the early 1940s, "The East is Red":

> The East is Red, the sun rises.
> In China a Mao Zedong is born.
> He seeks the people's happiness.
> He is the people's Great Savior.[45]

By 1943, "the people's Great Savior" had managed to attain two important new political titles — Chairman of the Central Committee, and Chairman of the Politburo (the Central Committee's executive arm), and the cult of his person was reaching unprecedented heights. As an American reporter visiting Yanan during this period noted,

Chairman Mao was the object of "panegyrics [praise] of the most high-flown, almost nauseatingly slavish eloquence," even from fellow CCP leaders such as Zhou Enlai.[46]

BREAKDOWN OF THE SECOND UNITED FRONT

As Mao was gaining unquestioned supremacy within the Communist movement, international events appeared to be turning in China's favor in its long struggle against Japan. After the Japanese attack on its naval base at Pearl Harbor in December 1941, the United States declared war on Japan and entered World War II (1939–1945), which pitted the Allies (principally Britain, France, and the Soviet Union) against the Axis powers (Japan, Germany, and Italy). Both Mao and Chiang Kaishek believed that it was just a matter of time before the powerful U.S. military crushed Japan. Hence, both sides began to shift their attention from ousting the Japanese occupiers to building their own resources for the civil war that was sure to engulf China once Japan was routed. By this time, the Second United Front was all but dead in the wake of the Anhui Incident of January 1941. In that notorious episode, Nationalist forces viciously attacked a Communist army that the ever-suspicious Chiang worried was stationed too close to his former capital at Nanjing.

By the time the American atomic strike against Japan ended World War II in August 1945, the Communists had managed to build their movement to record strength under Mao's adept direction. The Red Army now numbered close to 1 million troops, and 19 Communist base areas with a population of perhaps 90 million were dispersed across northern and central China. Zealous political indoctrination and propaganda campaigns and a renewed policy of distributing farm fields from landlords to peasants had earned Mao the unswerving loyalty of many of those 90 million.

Despite the enormous gains made by the Communists during the war years, however, Chiang's troops were still three times as numerous as Mao's forces—and significantly better equipped—and all of far western and southern China, including the key financial center of Shanghai, were firmly under Nationalist control. Nonetheless, convinced of the absolute rightness of his cause, Mao did not despair. "Chiang Kaishek and his supporters," he declared, were merely "paper tigers." A paper tiger "looks terrible," he explained, "but in fact it isn't. . . . We have only millet [grain] plus rifles to rely on, but history will finally prove that our millet plus rifles is more powerful than Chiang Kaishek's airplanes plus tanks . . . The reason is simply this: The reactionaries represent reaction, we represent progress."[47]

CIVIL WAR

As Mao and Chiang prepared for war, the U.S. government was doing its best to try to avert a major military conflict in China. During the months preceding and following Japan's surrender, the administration of President Harry S. Truman attempted repeatedly to mediate between the Communists and the Nationalists. Viewing China as a potential ally and stabilizing force in the troubled Far East, Truman hoped to promote peace and democracy within Asia's largest country. The more moderate Chiang, he expected, would serve as China's new president, but the Communists would be permitted to participate in free nationwide elections.

Although Chiang and Mao gave lip service to the American peace initiative, it soon became clear that neither had any sincere interest in compromise. Both sought absolute control over China for themselves and their party. From August 1945 on, Mao and Chiang had scrambled to move their troops northward into the vast, mineral-rich region of Manchuria to ensure that their commanders were the ones to take the Japanese surrender and disarm the enemy, even as the two leaders participated in U.S.–led negotiations. U.S. airlifts of Nationalist troops to Manchuria permitted Chiang to stay a step ahead of Mao in taking over from the enemy forces. Nonetheless, when Red troops did at last arrive in Manchuria, they were secretly supplied with large quantities of captured Japanese weapons and ammunition by the Soviet troops who had occupied the region since the last days of World War II.

In mid-1946, Chiang, worried by the growing Communist presence in the economically and strategically vital region, launched a concerted campaign to push all Red troops out of Manchuria. Civil war—or the War of Liberation, as Mao called it—had begun in earnest. Outgunned and outnumbered, the Communists were forced to retreat north. Although the Communists suffered a string of humiliating defeats in southern Manchuria, they still managed to hold onto the northern portion of the region by establishing isolated base areas and winning mass support through political education and land redistribution programs—a strategy firmly grounded in Maoist principles.

Assisted by Long March veterans Zhu De, Zhou Enlai, Lin Biao, and Peng Dehuai, Mao assumed direct command of the Communists' military campaign from the start. His overriding goal during the first phase of the war was to expand his armies with peasant recruits—and Nationalist defectors, if possible. Ever the pragmatist, Mao carefully avoided positional warfare in Manchuria and in all parts of China until he was sure his forces were sufficiently strong to prevail.

As he had done during Chiang's encirclement campaigns of the early 1930s, during the first year of the War of Liberation Mao relied primarily on guerrilla tactics and gave priority to safeguarding precious manpower over preserving territory. In March 1947, he even allowed the Nationalists to capture his longtime headquarters at Yanan in Shaanxi province. At the same time, he made sure that every effort was made to mobilize the peasants living near Communist bases to assist his troops by forming local militias, spying, and providing transport and essential supplies. "People's war" was the name now given to Mao's brand of warfare, with its emphasis on both guerrilla tactics to weaken a militarily superior enemy piecemeal and political indoctrination and economic reform to gain mass support.

By the summer of 1947, Mao's largely defensive doctrine of people's war was starting to reap encouraging results for the People's Liberation Army (PLA), as the Communist forces were now called. After reaching a high point with the capture of Yanan, Chiang's fortunes had begun a steady decline. By the late spring of 1947, the Nationalists had already lost 1 million soldiers, many of them defectors to the PLA. In contrast to the primarily volunteer forces of the PLA, most of the Nationalist rank and file had been forced into military service by press gangs that traveled from village to village, kidnapping men from their families and fields. To prevent them from escaping, the conscripts were roped together on marches. Many suffered from malnutrition because corrupt officers stole their rice rations, substituting sand for the pilfered grain. In the PLA, the common soldier was treated more humanely, rations were more plentiful, and morale was significantly higher.

Nor was it only within the armed forces that Chiang and his Nationalist cause were losing support during 1947;

the civilian population was also becoming increasingly disgruntled with the runaway inflation and rampant corruption that plagued most Nationalist-controlled areas in China. To a growing number of Chinese, including many in the middle class, the Communists and their program of economic and political reform appeared as the nation's best hope for the future. The CCP, not the Nationalists, seemed to be the party of modernization and effective, honest leadership.

By the last half of 1947, the PLA had grown to 2 million soldiers as a result of Nationalist defections and the recruitment of increasing numbers of volunteers from Communist-governed areas. For the first time in the long struggle between the Reds and the Nationalists, manpower ratios were starting to favor the Communists. In September 1947, Mao announced that the PLA was at last ready to launch a nationwide counteroffensive in which guerrilla operations would escalate into large-scale, conventional warfare. "Be sure to fight no battle unprepared," and in every engagement fight relentlessly, allowing the foe no chance to recoup, he admonished his troops.[48]

The rapid success of the new PLA offensive surprised even Mao. By November 1948, Lin Biao, one of Mao's finest generals, had managed to conquer Manchuria. In keeping with Mao's admonition to "fight no battle you are not sure of winning," Lin's first campaigns were directed against isolated Nationalist divisions.[49] After a series of morale-building victories, he moved against larger NP commands, carefully choosing those commands based on information provided by Mao. According to Mao, effective commanders "familiarize ourselves with all aspects of the enemy situation."[50] Hence, early in the Civil War, Mao began compiling a detailed catalogue of the Nationalist Army. According to the journalist Harrison Salisbury, Mao's record included "a dossier on every commander and every military unit,

By 1947, the tide of civil war in China had turned in favor of the Communists. Faced with military defeats and an increased number of defections from his army, Chiang Kaishek authorized bands of Nationalist troops to capture local villagers and force them into a sort of slave labor.

down to battalion level, sometimes even to company grade," making it "a tool of extraordinary utility. . . . Every Red Army officer knew which commanders were quick to break and run, which units were badly trained and would fall apart under a hard blow, which generals were professionals."[51]

After routing the Nationalists in Manchuria, with

Chiang losing huge quantities of captured weapons—
many of them American-supplied—and hundreds of
thousands of his best troops, the Communists pushed
southward into central China. Advancing with astonish-
ing rapidity, they surrounded and captured one city after
another. Morale within Chiang's forces plummeted as
PLA victories at the vital railroad junction of Huai-Hai
and the city of Tianjin put them in full retreat. About the
same time that Tianjin fell in January 1949, Communist
forces rolled into Beijing. In the spring of 1949, the PLA
finally breached Nationalist defenses on the great Yangtze
River dividing northern and southern China. Chiang had
hoped the United States would send troops to help him
hold the strategically critical river. The Truman administration, however, although it had donated 2 billion
dollars in financial aid to Chiang's side since 1945,
refused to go so far as to commit American soldiers to
saving the collapsing Nationalist regime.

In April 1949, Nanjing, Chiang's capital on the southern
banks of the Yangtze, fell to the Communists, with Shanghai
capitulating in May, and Changsha in August. Although
portions of southwestern China remained under Nationalist
control, Communist victory was now assured. On September 30, the Central Committee named Mao Chairman of
the People's Republic of China and the next day, he stood
on Beijing's Tiananmen Gate to officially announce the
founding of the new Communist Chinese state. Two
months later, Chiang Kaishek abandoned Mainland China
for the island of Taiwan, taking with him his air force,
navy, the remnants of his army, as well as all the government's gold and silver reserves.

Able and determined leadership on the part of Mao
and his top generals, high morale within the PLA ranks,
excellent mobility, and widespread civilian support all
contributed to the Communist victory in 1949. So, too,

many historians believe, did the ineptitude, arrogance, and corruption that beset much of the Nationalist political and military leadership. With the War of Liberation finally over, Mao was ready to turn his attention from military matters to the challenge of remaking the economy, government, and society of his homeland according to his Communist principles. "The achievement of nationwide victory is only the first step in a Long March," he warned his fellow party members. "It is silly to pride ourselves on this one step. What is more worthy of pride lies still ahead . . . The Chinese revolution is a great revolution, but the road beyond is longer and the work to come greater and more arduous . . . We should be capable not only of destroying the old world. We must also be capable of creating the new." [52]

6

Confronting Challenges at Home and Abroad: 1949–1959

In October 1949, Mao and his closest lieutenants, including Zhou Enlai and Liu Shaoqi, another former Long Marcher, began tackling the enormous task of rebuilding China following 12 years of war. With China's economy and transportation system in a shambles, Mao and his advisors concurred that financial assistance from abroad was essential. In addition to economic aid, they also hoped to obtain military protection for their war-weakened nation. Consequently, within weeks of taking power, Mao headed for the Soviet Union to negotiate with its leader of the past 25 years, Joseph Stalin. Mao probably did not relish the prospect of having to ask the Soviet dictator for aid. Yet with anti-Communist sentiment growing throughout

After Chiang Kaishek and the remaining Nationalist forces had fled to Taiwan, Mao (seen here in jeep) and his lieutenants began to tackle the task of rebuilding a country that had been ravaged by a dozen years of bitter warfare.

the world as "Cold War" rivalry between the Soviet Union and the United States deepened, Mao probably felt he had nowhere else to turn.

Despite their shared commitment to Communism, relations between Stalin and Mao were strained in 1949.

Although the PLA had received some assistance from Moscow in its struggle against the Nationalists, primarily in the form of captured Japanese weapons from Soviet-occupied Manchuria, Mao had hoped for far more support from Stalin during the Civil War. Stalin, however, was not about to waste Soviet resources on what he believed to be a hopeless cause. At the end of World War II, convinced that the PLA had little chance of prevailing over Chiang Kaishek's forces, Stalin tried to persuade Mao to reunite with the Nationalists. Even when the PLA was on the brink of victory in August 1949, Stalin was still negotiating with Chiang—not Mao—for Soviet mineral rights in western China.

In late 1949, concerned above all else with the survival of the new PRC, Mao was prepared to forget his past differences with the haughty Soviet dictator. Following nine weeks of negotiations in Moscow, Mao finally persuaded Stalin to sign a Treaty of Friendship, Alliance, and Mutual Assistance. According to the agreement, China and the Soviet Union were obliged to come to one another's defense in case of attack. In addition to the pledge of military assistance, Mao also managed to wring out of Stalin $300 million in credits over the next five years. In return for this loan (which was less than the USSR had recently awarded Poland, a country one-twentieth the size of China), the Soviets were guaranteed important economic privileges in the PRC, including mineral rights in western China and control over a key Manchurian railway line. Although "these concessions touched the core of his national pride," Ross Terrill writes, "Mao felt he had no alternative but to bow a knee before Stalin."[53] That 300 million dollars in credit was better than nothing, and nothing was what Mao knew he could expect from the United States and the rest of the capitalist "Free World."

THE KOREAN WAR BEGINS

When Mao, treaty in hand, returned to Beijing in the winter of 1950, he was anxious to focus his attention on rebuilding China's devastated economy and infrastructure. The last thing he needed was a costly and distracting new war. Yet, within less than a year, hundreds of thousands of Chinese troops would be fighting and dying in one of the bloodiest conflicts in history—the Korean War.

The Korean War had its roots in the immediate post–World War II period when U.S. and Soviet troops occupied the Korean Peninsula following its liberation from Japanese rule. The two superpowers agreed to divide Korea into separate areas of authority, with the Soviets occupying the region north of the 38th parallel, and the United States predominating south of the parallel. By mid-1949, American and Russian troops had departed the Peninsula, yet their influence lingered on. In the wake of their occupation, Korea was now split into two hostile countries—anti-Communist, pro-Western South Korea below the 38th parallel, and Communist, pro-Soviet North Korea above.

Kim Il-Sung, North Korea's ambitious dictator, was determined to reunite the fragmented Peninsula under his own rule. With the assistance of North Korea's closest ally, the Soviet Union, Kim transformed his nation's army into a well-equipped fighting force. On June 25, 1950, he launched an all-out, surprise attack southward across the 38th parallel. Convinced the South Korean masses would unite behind their Communist "liberators," Kim was confident that the war would soon be over.

Kim's bold invasion came as no surprise to Mao. By the spring of 1950, Kim had alerted Mao regarding his intention to move against the South some time in the future. What did shock Mao, however, was the response of the U.S. government to the offensive. In January 1950, Truman indicated that the Korean Peninsula lay beyond the American defense line; yet within days of Kim's attack, he ordered American naval, air, and ground forces to come to the defense of South Korea. The signing of the Sino-Soviet Alliance in February 1950 as well as the massive military aide the USSR had been providing to North Korea apparently changed Truman's mind regarding the significance of East Asia in the Cold War between the Communist sphere and the Free World. Truman and his advisors now believed that Communist expansion in Korea and throughout the Far East must be strictly contained.

The U.S. forces were to fight in Korea under the banner of the United Nations, the international peacekeeping organization founded at the end of World War II. In the wake of Kim's invasion, the U.N. Security Council had passed a resolution calling for the cooperation of all members in repelling the attack, which it condemned as a violation of international peace. (Had he been present, the Council's Soviet delegate would surely have vetoed the resolution. However, he was boycotting the council to protest the granting of China's U.N. seat to Nationalist Taiwan instead of to the PRC.)

While the U.N. forces—comprised mostly of American troops—prepared for battle, the North Korean army was pushing rapidly southward. By late July, it occupied some 90 percent of South Korea, including Seoul, the capital. The South Korean army plus four divisions of U.S. troops that had been rushed to the Peninsula earlier that month were pressed into a tiny area on South Korea's southeastern tip known as the Pusan Perimeter. It seemed that Kim's dreams of a quick victory were coming true.

In mid-September of 1950, however, the tide began to turn in the Allies' favor when 80,000 U.S. Marines, under the direction of General Douglas MacArthur, staged a daring amphibious landing at Inchon, just west of Seoul

After 80,000 U.S. Marines under the direction of General Douglas MacArthur successfully landed at Inchon and began pushing through North Korea toward the Chinese border, Mao sent Chinese troops to intervene on behalf of the Communists.

and considerably north of the main battlefront. In a well-coordinated campaign, Allied forces then converged on Kim's army from the north and the south, where the now heavily reinforced U.S. and South Korean troops had burst out of the Pusan Perimeter. By early October, Kim's army had been shattered, and the U.N. forces were pushing across the 38th parallel into North Korea. Soon Allied troops were closing in on the Yalu River, the border between northeastern China and North Korea.

MAO'S WAR DECISION
With U.S. forces approaching China's border and the collapse of North Korea apparently imminent, Mao decided China must enter the conflict. Although historians

disagree as to exactly when Mao committed the PLA to defending North Korea, many scholars now believe that he had been contemplating military intervention on the Peninsula ever since the United States and the U.N. proclaimed their determination to repel Kim's invasion in late June. By July, the historian Chen Jian reports, Mao was already taking steps to prepare the PLA for a potential military operation in Korea, moving 250,000 Chinese troops into position along the Yalu River.

As Mao was readying China's armed forces for battle during the summer of 1950, he was also preparing its citizenry for the daunting prospect of another war with a nationwide propaganda campaign dubbed the "Great Movement to Resist America and Assist Korea." With "beating American arrogance" as its chief slogan, Mao's crusade was designed to stir up mass resentment against the "U.S. imperialists" whom he accused of orchestrating the Allied campaign to meddle in Korea's internal affairs.[54]

Yet, despite Mao's fervent propaganda campaign, by early autumn, Chinese troops had still not crossed the border into North Korea. During the three months following Kim's invasion, Mao and his top military advisors were locked in a debate over when—if at all—China should join the fray. Mao's commanders strongly advised caution, arguing that China should not enter the war until the Soviets offered a clear guarantee of military support. Since the PLA was far less well equipped than the U.N. forces, Soviet military assistance was critical, they argued.

Stalin's unwillingness to clarify what—if any—support he would give the Chinese should they choose to fight troubled Mao's commanders throughout the summer. Long before fighting erupted on the Peninsula, the Soviet government had been providing military aid to North

Korea in the form of supplies and advisers. Yet Stalin was reluctant to send Soviet troops to Korea, apparently because he feared such a move might lead to an all-out war between the USSR and its powerful Cold War rival, the United States. He was more than happy, however, to have China enter the conflict on Kim's side, especially after the successful Allied landing at Inchon. The next month, as the U.N. forces were pushing their way ever farther into North Korea, Stalin finally seemed ready to offer Mao the aid his commanders were convinced the PLA required in Korea. If China entered the war, Stalin implied to Mao, the Soviets would provide weapons and other supplies as well as full air cover, which the PLA, with its woefully outdated warplanes and antiaircraft equipment, desperately needed.

On October 2, Mao used Stalin's promise of assistance and his own considerable authority to persuade his CCP colleagues to back intervention in Korea. Even when Stalin, claiming that his air units were not yet "properly prepared" for the operation, reneged a week later on providing air support to the Chinese forces, Mao held firm, ordering additional troops to the Chinese-Korean border and placing them under the command of the respected Long March and Civil War veteran, Peng Duhai.[55] So that China could escape the official status of belligerent, Mao dubbed Peng's army the Chinese People's Volunteers.

Why was Mao so determined to enter the Korean War, despite the lack of Soviet air support and the objections of his military advisers? According to many historians, national security concerns were at the core of Mao's decision to fight, and specifically, his apprehensions regarding the stridently anti-Communist United States. Convinced that the U.S. government sought not only to contain Communism in Asia but also to roll it back, he feared that if North Korea buckled before the Allies, the PRC would be their next logical target. On the battlefields of Korea, Mao believed, the PRC must show the United States and its allies that China possessed both the will and the military capability to defend itself from foreign interference.

MAO INTERVENES

On the night of October 19, 1950, as U.S. forces continued their march into North Korea, 300,000 Chinese People's Volunteers began crossing the Yalu. By preserving complete radio silence and dimming all vehicle lights, the troops managed to avoid detection by U.S. intelligence forces for days. On October 25, Chinese units made contact with U.N. advance troops near the Yalu, and fighting ensued. Yet after several more skirmishes with enemy advance forces during the following week, the Chinese abruptly disappeared.

Although Mao had advised Truman through China's Indian ambassador earlier in October that his troops would intervene if the U.S. advance toward the Yalu continued, both Truman and MacArthur dismissed the warning as propaganda. As of early November, MacArthur still had no idea that several hundred thousand Chinese soldiers had already infiltrated North Korea; he thought the number of Chinese troops in Korea was far smaller. Consequently, after the Chinese that had skirmished with his advance units since October 25 suddenly retreated, MacArthur regrouped his forces for a major attack along the northern front near the Yalu. All of North Korea would be under U.N. control by Christmas, the general confidently declared.

On November 25, with the bulk of U.N. forces well inside North Korea and their supply lines stretched thin,

As U.S. marines threatened to cross the Yalu River, Mao launched a massive counteroffensive, sending waves of Chinese soldiers across the border into North Korea. Allied forces, already stretched thin and unprepared for the harsh Korean winter, were soon forced to retreat.

the Communists launched a sudden and vigorous counteroffensive. Using night attacks and huge "human wave" assaults to overwhelm and demoralize their far better equipped opponents, the Chinese and North Koreans won a string of impressive victories. Outnumbered and woefully unprepared for the bitter North Korean winter, the Allied troops were pushed farther and farther south. Mao, emboldened by the Communist triumphs, ordered Peng to cross the 38th parallel. By New Year's Eve, Chinese and North Korean forces had pressed into South Korea and recaptured Seoul.

During these heady first months of Chinese participation in the war, Mao exercised hands-on leadership of the army's campaigns from Beijing, "following them with meticulous attention, intervening countless times with his own orders or tactical suggestions," writes Jonathan Spence.[56] During one five-day period of especially heavy fighting, notes Ross Terrill, Mao sent off "no fewer than 18 cables with detailed instructions to Peng Dehuai at the front."[57] Mao made the decision to involve Chinese troops in Korea in the first place; now he was determined to maintain as much control as possible over the course of the fighting.

But there was little Mao or his commanders could do in January 1951 when the Communist push southward began to lose its momentum in the face of superior Allied firepower and their own overextended supply lines. By early April, the Allies had retaken Seoul and were again crossing the 38th parallel into North Korea. That same month, Truman relieved MacArthur of his command after the general demanded that the fighting be taken into China itself, a course of action Truman feared would bring the USSR into the conflict and lead to a third world war.

Over the next months, the Korean War settled into a stalemate, with the front-line eventually stabilizing close to the 38th parallel. Peace talks commenced in mid-1951 but dragged on for two more years. Ironically, the armistice agreement finally signed by the two sides on July 27, 1953, left the border between North and South Korea about where it had been before the war began.

CONSEQUENCES OF THE KOREAN WAR

The Korean War proved costly for the PRC, particularly in the human toll it exacted. Largely as a result of the Chinese People's Volunteers' inadequate air cover and "human wave" tactics, some 900,000 Chinese died in the war; among the casualties was Mao's 28-year-old son by his second wife, Yang Kaihui. Mao and the PRC also paid dearly for their Korean venture in other ways. In June 1950, Mao expected to soon reunite Nationalist-controlled Taiwan with the mainland—by force, if necessary. At the outbreak of the Korean War, however, Truman ordered the U.S. Seventh Fleet to the Taiwan Straits separating Chiang's island refuge from the PRC, signaling that Taiwan, like South Korea, was now part of the U.S.

Mao Crushes a Rebellion in Tibet

Although the region of Tibet enjoyed virtual independence for many centuries and its inhabitants are ethnically and culturally distinct from the Han, who comprise the majority of China's population, Mao and his CCP colleagues were convinced that Tibet rightfully belonged to the People's Republic. In the autumn of 1951, therefore, Mao ordered the People's Liberation Army to occupy Tibet. Soon after, the supreme Tibetan political and religious ruler, the Dalai Lama, signed an agreement with the Chinese government. According to the agreement, Tibet would become part of the PRC, but its people would be allowed to retain their traditional religious, social, and political structures.

As the decade progressed, however, the Beijing regime interfered more and more in Tibet's internal affairs, particularly after Mao launched his Great Leap Forward in 1958. In 1959, the embittered Tibetans revolted. Acting under Mao's orders, the PLA quickly and brutally crushed the rebellion, and the Dalai Lama and many of his leading supporters fled to neighboring India. To Mao's dismay, the New Delhi government strongly sympathized with the Tibetans, even permitting the Dalai Lama and his associates to create a government-in-exile in India. Back in Tibet, the insurgents and anyone suspected of aiding and abetting them were made to pay dearly for the failed rebellion. In the wake of the revolt, the Chinese all but destroyed Tibet's traditional political, social, and religious systems, torching scores of Buddhist monasteries and temples and exiling to labor camps or executing thousands of Tibetans.

defense zone. Mao had little choice but to put his plans to "liberate" Taiwan on hold. In addition to thwarting Mao's plans for Taiwan, the United States exacted another heavy toll from the PRC in retribution for its actions in Korea: a trade embargo, which was supported by most of the West. The harsh embargo would last for two decades, significantly hampering China's economic development.

Yet the effects of the Korean War were not entirely negative for Mao. That the PRC had not only stood up to the powerful United States but actually succeeded in fighting its forces to a standstill brought China's new Communist regime increased prestige and credibility at

Mao and the Taiwan Crisis of 1958

In 1954, Mao ordered the shelling of Matsu and Quemoy (also known as Jinmen), small Nationalist-controlled islands in the Taiwan Straits off the coast of southern China. Mao halted the artillery attacks only after U.S. President Dwight D. Eisenhower announced that the United States would defend the islands. Four years later, in August 1958, just as he was launching the Great Leap Forward, Mao again decided to shell Quemoy and Matsu. Undoubtedly, he wanted to test the continuing U.S. commitment to Chiang Kaishek and his Nationalist government on Taiwan with this new bombardment. Some historians, however, speculate that Mao's decision to shell Quemoy and Matsu in the summer of 1958 was also linked to his desire to mobilize popular support for the demanding Great Leap Forward policies, particularly the unpopular rural communes. Mao sought to create a crisis situation in the Taiwan Straits, these scholars argue, because he was convinced that by promoting nationalistic fervor and a sense of unity, international crises would motivate the masses to submit to government policies. After President Eisenhower strongly reiterated his determination to defend Quemoy and Matsu in 1958, even threatening air and naval action against the People's Republic if the shellings continued, Mao backed down and the crisis passed.

home and abroad. At home, the war further strength-
ened Mao's own already dominant position within the
party and the country, leaving him virtually untouchable,
according to Chen Jian. Abroad, the Chinese military's
impressive performance also won new respect for Mao,
particularly from the Soviet Union. If Moscow had new
regard for the Chinese leader after the Korean War, however, Mao's respect for the Soviet leadership decreased
during the course of the conflict. First, Stalin reneged on
his pledge to provide full air cover to the Chinese troops.
Then, following Stalin's death in March 1953, his successors compelled the PRC to reimburse the Soviet treasury
at full market price for each and every Soviet rifle and
grenade the People's Volunteers used in the war. This
miserliness, Mao believed, indicated a shameful lack of
solidarity with the international Communist community
on the part of his comrades in Moscow.

THE GREAT LEAP FORWARD

With the end of the Korean War, Mao refocused his
attention on China's economy. That year, he initiated the
Five-Year Economic Plan to spur development of industry. Mao also stepped up the program he had begun
before the war for reforming China's ancient agricultural
system by seizing landlord property and redistributing it
to the peasants.

By the late 1950s, the Chinese economy was showing
signs of recovery. Mao, however, was deeply dissatisfied
with the pace of its growth. As Harrison Salisbury
explains, Mao reasoned that since "it had taken the Red
Army only 15 years from the Long March to the conquest
of all China, then economic development shouldn't take so
long." [58] To speed up development, in 1958 Mao concocted
a radical new plan based on what he considered to be his

nation's greatest natural resource—its vast population. By harnessing the enormous energy of China's masses, Mao was confident that China would soon leap ahead of the West and the Soviet Union in its industrial and agricultural output. Accordingly, he called his new program the Great Leap Forward.

In the industrial realm, the Leap emphasized increasing steel output, calling for sharply stepped-up production in China's few existing steel factories. To meet the Chairman's high production quotas, factory operatives were even prodded to sleep at their machines. Mao's plan to expand China's steel output also called for creating a brand-new source of steel production in the form of small-scale "backyard furnaces" to be constructed in villages all over the Chinese countryside and manned by peasants.

In the agricultural realm, Mao demanded a complete reorganization of the farming population. Assigning the peasantry to vast communes, he believed, would both spur agricultural output and hasten the PRC's evolution into a truly Communist state by abolishing private land ownership. By 1959, more than 25,000 communes, each composed of some 20,000 persons, had been established throughout rural China. Life in the huge communes was vastly different from anything the Chinese masses had ever known. Instead of living and working in family units, peasants were assigned to dormitories and work teams. So that married women might be full participants in the agricultural work force, the communes included day care centers and canteens for collective dining. In the fields, men and women labored together in military formation, clothed in identical blue trousers and tunics.

Many Chinese—from government officials worried about its heavy reliance on ramshackle backyard furnaces to increase steel production, to peasants loath to surrender

With the Korean War resolved, Mao again turned to revitalizing China's economy. In a plan to increase steel output, Mao proposed the creation of a decentralized system of small "backyard furnaces" that would be located in villages and operated by the local peasants. This steel worker is employed at a plant in Anshan, in northern China.

their land—were dismayed by the Great Leap Forward. Yet no one dared to speak out against the Chairman and his revolutionary program. By 1958, an atmosphere of fear permeated the PRC. Criticizing Mao or his policies was dangerous, the Chinese had discovered; it could result in the loss of your job, your reputation, or even your freedom.

When the Chairman launched his Great Leap experiment, the PRC was in the grips of a repressive, government-sponsored crusade known as the "Anti-Rightest" campaign. Started in 1957, the Anti-Rightest campaign developed in response to one of Mao's earlier experiments, the "Hundred Flowers Movement." In the Hundred Flowers Movement, Mao encouraged China's citizens—especially its intellectuals—to voice their concerns regarding the infant Communist regime. Expecting mild criticism at worst, Mao was incensed when many people expressed serious doubts regarding the course that the revolution had taken thus far. Grimly determined to quash any challenge to his authority, Mao branded his critics as "rightists" and "reactionaries"—two of the worst epithets in the Communist lexicon. Between 1957 and 1959, hundreds of thousands of accused rightists were publicly denounced and hauled off to prison or to forced labor camps.

In the wake of the brutal Anti-Rightist campaign, most Chinese kept quiet, even when it became evident that Mao's Great Leap policies were floundering. Owing in large measure to the backyard furnaces, China's steel output did increase in 1958, but most of the steel being forged in the makeshift smelters was of such low quality as to be virtually worthless. As peasants neglected their fields to run the crude furnaces, agricultural output plummeted. Many of those peasants who remained in the fields worked less hard than when they had tilled their own plots because they knew that under the new Communist system, more work would not bring more food or other material benefits for themselves or their families. By the autumn of 1958, agricultural output had already dropped to the point that food shortages were appearing in many parts of the country.

When the PRC's top leadership met to evaluate the Great Leap's first year in July 1959, Peng Duhai, commander of the Chinese "Volunteers" in the Korean War and defense minister since 1954, felt he could no longer remain silent. Mao's experiment was failing, Peng bluntly declared. On a recent tour of the countryside, he reported, he had observed widespread hunger and officials who routinely over-reported production figures. Moreover, Peng said, the peasants were fed up with the new policies; they detested the mass dining halls, barracks-like dormitories, and virtual annihilation of family life that went along with the communes.

Mao was infuriated by Peng's criticisms. If the CCP leadership sided with Peng against him, Mao stormed, "I will go to the countryside to lead the peasants to overthrow the government." Glaring at the military personnel present, he threatened, "If those of you in the Liberation Army won't follow me, I will go and find a [new] Red Army."[59] Faced with Mao's wrath, not a single senior official supported Peng. Branding Peng a capitalist and a rightist, Mao dismissed him from all his official posts, appointing another close military associate from his Long March days, Lin Biao, as China's new defense minister.

By 1960, however, even Mao had to admit that the Great Leap was faltering. That year, China suffered the worst famine in its recorded history, when bad weather compounded the chaos and waste created by the Great Leap's flawed economic and social policies. It has been estimated that between 1958 and 1961, upward of 30 million Chinese died from starvation. Mao's revolutionary vision for a stronger, more prosperous China had descended into a nightmare.

An Era of Turmoil:
1960–1976

The collapse of the Great Leap Forward took a toll on Mao's once-paramount influence within the PRC. During the early 1960s, Deng Xiaoping, another former Long Marcher, and Liu Shaoqi (now head of state, although Mao retained the more important position of CCP Chairman) instituted a series of pragmatic reforms designed to shore up the tottering economy. Breaking with Mao's radical policies, Liu and Deng's new program called for abolishing backyard steel mills, scaling back communes, and using profit incentives to increase worker productivity. Mao feared that his revolutionary vision for China and his own authority were in grave peril.

Mao's "Great Leap Forward" had proven disastrous. Several leading Chinese officials had to struggle to save the nation's faltering economy. Among them was Deng Xiaoping (just right of center), seen here in a 1963 photograph when he was part of a Chinese Communist delegation to the Soviet Union.

MAO FIGHTS BACK: LEARNING FROM THE PLA

Determined to revive both his radical policies and his faltering influence, in the early 1960s Mao began building a new power base for himself within the PLA, which had been under the control of Mao's zealous supporter, Lin Biao, since Peng Duhai's fall. Mao was confident that China's new defense minister was fiercely loyal to him and his ideals, including his conception of how the army ought to be run. Peng Duhai, hoping to transform the PLA into a more conventional and professional fighting force, had broken with Maoist principles by introducing ranks into the army and de-emphasizing political indoctrination. Once in office, Lin Biao promptly reversed

Peng's reforms, abolishing ranks and stressing a vigorous political indoctrination program that focused almost exclusively on Mao's ideas.

As part of his political education program, in 1964 Lin collected quotations from Mao's key writings and speeches and published them in a single volume that became known as "The Little Red Book." Lin ordered every soldier to study the quotations carefully. The PLA, he proclaimed, would become a "great school of Mao Zedong's thought."[60] That same year, Mao launched a nationwide campaign exhorting all Chinese to "learn from the PLA." Mao's new crusade lauded the soldiers as

Mao and the Bomb

In August 1945, after the United States brought World War II to an end in the Pacific by dropping atomic bombs on the Japanese cities of Hiroshima and Nagasaki, Mao casually dismissed the new nuclear weapons as mere "paper tigers"—he said they appeared much more dangerous than they actually were. By the mid-1950s, however, Mao had reversed his stand on the A-bomb and committed the People's Republic to developing its own nuclear capability. Nuclear weapons, Mao now decided, served as a highly useful deterrent against those who feared them, including the PRC's most powerful enemy at the time, the United States. The PRC must join the nuclear club, he told foreign visitors, even though the financial cost to the struggling young nation would be enormous.

Although Moscow at first agreed to send advisors to China to help their Communist neighbor build an atomic bomb, by 1960 Russian leader Nikita Khrushchev had withdrawn the offer in the face of deteriorating Sino-Soviet relations. Nonetheless, with the help of a Chinese-American scientist who had been deported from the United States in the mid-1950s because of his Communist ties, the PRC forged ahead with its nuclear program. To Mao's immense satisfaction and pride, by 1964 the Chinese had managed to construct and successfully detonate their first A-bomb. Just 32 months later, the PRC exploded its first hydrogen bomb as well.

models of revolutionary zeal and virtue and called on China's civilians to emulate them, particularly by studying his own teachings. To assist the people in this endeavor, millions of copies of "The Little Red Book" were printed and distributed throughout the country.

The wide dissemination of "The Little Red Book" and other Maoist writings enhanced the Chairman's prestige among the masses, and especially among the youth who already idealized him as their nation's supreme revolutionary hero. The Maoist cult of personality that had first appeared in the 1940s flourished as the Chairman was exalted as China's "Great Teacher" and "Great Helmsman." The time was ripe for Mao to make the next move in his campaign to reassert his political sway: Mao would mobilize the masses, particularly the youth, to topple those in authority whom he believed had betrayed him and his revolutionary ideals by leading China down the "capitalist road." [61]

THE GREAT PROLETARIAN CULTURAL REVOLUTION

In May 1966, giant wall posters suddenly appeared at Beijing University exhorting students to rebel against the "capitalist roaders" corrupting the political and cultural life of Communist China with their rightist policies and values. After Mao publicly praised the inflammatory signs, university and high school students across the nation began putting up their own posters denouncing reactionary elements in the government and society. Soon, groups of students and other young people were donning khaki uniforms with red armbands and calling themselves Red Guards and champions of Mao Zedong and his revolutionary ideals.

In August, proclaiming it was good to "bombard the headquarters," Mao officially launched what he dubbed the "Great Proletarian Cultural Revolution" and endorsed the Red Guards as the radical new movement's vanguard.[62] Later that same month, the Chairman, outfitted in PLA fatigues, reviewed the Red Guards at an emotional rally in Beijing's Tiananmen Square. More than 1 million of his youth supporters waved and chanted "Red Book." Goaded on by Mao to expose and attack rightists and elitists everywhere, squads of Guards fanned out through China's cities and towns. Thanks to the PLA, which in essence requisitioned the national railroad system for the young radicals, the Red Guards traveled about China free of charge. Wherever they went, they left a trail of suspicion, hatred, and violence in their wake. Accused rightists—many of them principals, teachers, party officials, or others in positions of authority—were publicly humiliated, beaten, tortured, and often murdered or driven to suicide by Mao's adolescent thugs.

One of Mao's chief aims in launching the Cultural Revolution was to remove from power all those who had dared to question his ideas or authority. Among the movement's most prominent political victims were Liu Shaoqi and Deng Xiaoping, whose abandonment of the Great Leap Forward for more moderate economic and social policies was deeply resented by Mao. After enduring repeated public humiliations and severe physical abuse at the hands of the Red Guards, Liu was formally condemned as a counterrevolutionary and hauled off to prison. He eventually died there, after being denied medical treatment. Deng Xiaoping got off easier—he was sent to a remote part of Jiangxi province to labor in a small tractor-repair shop. Mao's old adversary Peng Duhai was also a major target of the Cultural Revolution. The former Long Marcher, distinguished Civil War general, and commander-in-chief of the Chinese army in

Mao's third wife, Jiang Qing, played an important part in the Cultural Revolution—crusading, often violently, to purge Chinese art, literature, and music of all foreign and "counterrevolutionary" influences.

Korea suffered more than 100 beatings by Mao's zealots before finally expiring at the age of 76.

Mao did not intend the Cultural Revolution to be only a crusade against certain party and government officials. As Shaun Breslin explains, for Mao the Revolution "was also an attack on all modes of thought and behavior that were not conducive to promoting the correct (i.e., Mao's) vision of socialism," including traditional Chinese religious beliefs and customs and all Western cultural imports from clothing styles to literature.[63] Early in the Revolution, Mao appointed his third wife, Jiang Qing, a former actress whom he married in 1938 after divorcing Hi Zizhen, to oversee a repressive and often violent crusade to cleanse

Chinese art, literature, music, and film of all "counter-revolutionary" or foreign influences.

By 1968, the fear and violence engendered by Mao's Great Proletarian Cultural Revolution had brought China to the brink of anarchy. Millions had been maimed or killed, factories and schools across the nation were shut down, the economy was in a shambles, and rival Red Guard units were battling one another to the death in the streets of China's cities. Mao had used the PLA to help launch his Revolution; now he looked to the military to rein it in. Under Lin Biao's direction, PLA units soon reestablished order, taking over factories and universities and forcibly transporting millions of Red Guards to remote rural villages to labor in the fields with the peasants. Mao also called on the PLA to rebuild China's fractured political system by forming revolutionary committees in cities and towns throughout the nation to coordinate local government, party, and military functions. By the end of the decade, life in China was finally beginning to return to normal, with most factories, schools, and government agencies slowly resuming their usual operations.

MAO RETHINKS HIS FOREIGN POLICY

Many scholars believe that the Cultural Revolution killed at least 4 million Chinese. It also returned to Mao Zedong the virtually undisputed authority he had enjoyed before the Great Leap Forward. In 1972, Mao used his revived power to carry out the last—and surely the most remarkable—foreign relations initiative of his long career: inviting the President of the United States to China.

Mao's willingness in the early 1970s to pursue rapprochement (cordial relations) with the United States, the PRC's archenemy for over two decades, had everything to do with China's relationship with the post–World War II era's other superpower, the Soviet Union. Relations between the Communist neighbors had begun to sour noticeably in the mid-1950s, when Mao publicly criticized Stalin's successor, Nikita Khrushchev, for seeking détente with the West. Khrushchev struck back at the Chairman over the next five years, first ridiculing his Great Leap Forward policies, then pulling all Soviet technical advisors out of the PRC, and finally refusing to support China in its brief border war with India in 1962.

From the early 1960s onward, Mao lashed out repeatedly at the Soviet leadership in his writings and speeches, accusing Khrushchev and his colleagues of being self-serving bureaucrats who had betrayed Marx and Lenin's revolutionary ideals. By 1964, the rupture between the two Communist neighbors had become irreversible. Five years later, in March 1969, Sino-Soviet tensions actually developed into armed conflict when Russian and Chinese troops clashed over disputed border areas in China's far northeast.

In the wake of the border clashes, Mao became convinced that the USSR posed a greater threat to China's national security than its old foe, the United States. Genuinely concerned about a Soviet nuclear attack on the PRC, Mao turned to the one nation in the world militarily powerful enough to act as a counterweight to the USSR. Meanwhile, the U.S. government, under the leadership of President Richard M. Nixon and his national security adviser, Henry Kissinger, also sought an adjustment in the current global balance of power. Just as Mao hoped to play the American card against his former Communist ally, Nixon and Kissinger hoped to play the Chinese card against their Soviet rivals. Thus, in 1971 the Nixon administration signaled its readiness to talk to Beijing by loosening the long-standing American trade embargo on China and supporting admission of the PRC to the United Nations.

In February 1972, Nixon traveled the 16,000 miles from Washington, D.C. to Beijing to meet with Mao. During the visit, Mao and Nixon (or the "God of Plague and War," as the Chinese press liked to call the U.S. President prior to 1971) agreed to start sending diplomats to serve in each other's capitals, although not one official

Mao and the Vietnam War

For nearly a century, Vietnam, China's neighbor to the south, was a colony of France. Following World War II, Vietnamese armies under the leadership of the Communist leader Ho Chi Minh battled the French to secure their nation's independence. After several years of harsh fighting, in 1954 France finally withdrew from Vietnam, which, like Korea, split into a Communist-governed North and an anti-Communist, pro-Western South. Soon, North Vietnamese guerrillas began infiltrating the South in order to "liberate" it.

By 1965, the guerrillas had made significant inroads and the United States, as determined as ever to contain Communist expansion, began intervening massively in the war on South Vietnam's side. Since the end of the Korean War in 1953, Mao had provided supplies and military advisers to North Vietnam, aid that increased significantly as U.S. involvement in the war escalated during the mid-1960s. In 1969, however, Mao drastically cut Chinese aid to North Vietnam, pulling out virtually all the engineering and antiaircraft units he had sent there in the mid-1960s. Many historians believe Mao was angered and worried by the growing closeness between the Soviet Union (his new archenemy) and the North Vietnamese government during the late 1960s. Mao's actions in Vietnam may also have been influenced by his growing interest in rapprochement with the United States and the fact that by 1969, it already appeared that South Vietnam and its American allies would probably lose the war, anyway. (In 1975, two years after a cease-fire was declared in Vietnam, South Vietnam fell to the North, and Vietnam was reunited under Communist rule.)

representative from either nation had traveled to the capital of the other since 1949.[64] "It had been an extraordinary shift in policy by Mao, to upend the strident attacks on U.S. imperialism that had flooded China's airwaves and newspapers for decades," writes Jonathan Spence, "and it is proof of the extraordinary power that Mao knew he had over his own people."[65] Within months of Nixon's momentous visit, however, the 78-year-old Mao suffered an apparent stroke and the power he had labored so assiduously to regain during the Cultural Revolution began to slip away from him once more.

MAO'S FINAL YEARS

In light of Mao's grave health problems, the question of who would succeed the PRC's longtime ruler became pressing. In 1969, Mao had appointed as his successor Lin Biao, his most devoted supporter during the Cultural Revolution and the difficult years preceding it. Mao, however, seldom trusted anyone for long. Soon he began to fret that Lin was a power-hungry opportunist and far less committed to Mao and his revolutionary program than he had once believed. Matters finally came to a head in late 1971, when the bodies of Lin Biao and several of his family members were discovered in a remote area of Mongolia following a mysterious airplane accident. Few hard facts have emerged regarding the incident, but after a lengthy and unexplained period of silence regarding Lin's demise, the Beijing government claimed that Lin's airplane had run out of fuel and crashed as he fled China following a botched assassination attempt on Mao.

With Lin out of the picture, Zhou Enlai, who had somehow avoided being purged during the Cultural Revolution, seemed the obvious choice to succeed Mao. However, in 1972, the same year Mao suffered his stroke,

Zhou discovered that he had a fatal form of cancer. Consequently, at Zhou's urging, Mao brought back to Beijing the disgraced Deng Xiaoping for the purpose of grooming him as his new successor. This infuriated Jiang Qing and the ultra-leftist group that had formed around Mao's wife during the Cultural Revolution. After a persistent campaign, Jiang and her followers finally convinced Mao that his heir apparent had not been rehabilitated by his years in exile and was still committed to steering China away from the radical path Mao had envisioned for his homeland. Shortly after Zhou's death in early 1976, Mao again dismissed Deng, replacing him with a quiet-spoken and relatively unknown Party official named Hua Guofeng. A few months later the ailing 82-year-old Chairman slipped into a coma.

Just after midnight on September 9, 1976, Mao Zedong died. According to his personal physician, during his final years Mao suffered from serious lung and heart ailments as well as Lou Gehrig's disease, a rare and debilitating neurological disease. After much debate among the CCP leadership, it was determined that the Chairman's emaciated body should be mummified (as Lenin's corpse had been following his death a half-century earlier), encased in a clear crystal coffin, and placed on public view in a huge marble mausoleum situated "close to the people" in the heart of Tiananmen Square.[66]

AFTER MAO

Within weeks of Mao's death, Jiang Qing, who had hoped to succeed her husband, was arrested along with her top supporters by a coalition of military and political leaders led by Hua Guofeng. Soon, however, Hua found himself sidelined by none other than the twice-purged Deng Xiaoping. Over the next two decades, Deng focused

Mao's final great act was to begin to repair the damaged relations between China and the United States. His health, however, had already begun to fail, and on September 9, 1976, Mao Zedong died. His body is interred here, at Beijing's Tiananmen Square.

on modernizing China's economy and infrastructure and expanding its trade and cultural relations with the international community. He instituted a number of far-reaching reforms, including dissolving the commune system and permitting peasants to farm for personal profit. Since Deng's death in 1997, his successors have continued his moderate policies, policies that stand in sharp contrast to Mao's revolutionary vision for the Communist state he had done so much to help create.

Despite the government's abandonment of most of his economic and social policies, however, nearly three decades after his death, Mao's presence still pervades the PRC, where he remains the central and most revered symbol of Communist China's identity. The majority of Chinese—from top party officials on down—now concur that Mao's leadership from the launching of the Great Leap Forward in the late 1950s through the Cultural Revolution of the 1960s was marked by grave errors and excesses. As costly as the debacles of the Great Leap and Cultural Revolution may have been, however, most believe that Mao's indispensable contributions to the Communists' struggle to liberate their nation from Japanese imperialism and Nationalist elitism far overshadow the Chairman's later failings.

Indeed, few scholars would deny Mao a leading role in the Communist victory of 1949. Other military and political figures including Zhou Enlai, Zhu De, and Lin Biao played vital roles in the Communist crusade to win China. Yet, as the Red Army/PLA's chief military strategist and the Communist movement's paramount political leader by the mid-1930s, Mao truly was the father of China's Communist Revolution.

From the time he proclaimed the establishment of the People's Republic on October 1, 1949, until his death 27 years later, Mao was also China's chief military and political policy maker, responsible for making and breaking alliances with foreign powers, sending hundreds of thousands of Chinese soldiers to fight in the Korean War, and using the PLA to encourage—and then to stifle— the violence and chaos of the Cultural Revolution. Perhaps most importantly, as the PRC's top leader, Mao was responsible for his homeland's metamorphosis from the humiliated, weak China of 1949 into a global superpower, a transformation symbolized by the 16,000-mile sojourn of the leader of the Western World—U.S. President Richard Nixon—to negotiate with Mao in Beijing in 1972. Despite his numerous faults and costly mistakes, Mao Zedong may at least be credited with this one major accomplishment: Under Mao's rule, China regained its self-respect and the respect of the world. China, as Mao himself once put it, "stood up."[67]

Spelling Chinese Words in English: Pinyin versus Wade-Giles

Several different systems for spelling Chinese names and words using the Roman alphabet have been developed over the years. Up until the last decades of the twentieth century, the most popular of these was the Wade-Giles system. In 1979, the People's Republic of China officially adopted a new and more phonetically accurate program for Romanizing Chinese words called the Pinyin system. Although this book uses the Pinyin system, names familiar in the West in their pre-Pinyin spellings appear in those forms; for example, Chiang Kaishek, Sun Yatsen, Hong Kong, Canton, Tibet, and Yangtze.

Since students doing research on Mao and China will probably encounter older texts—and even a few newer ones—that use the Wade-Giles system for translating Chinese words into English, the following chart provides both the Pinyin and Wade-Giles forms for many of the personal and place names included in this book.

WADE-GILES	PINYIN
Ch'en Tu-hsiu	Chen Duxiu
Ch'ing	Qing
Chiang Ching	Jiang Qing
Chou En-lai	Zhou Enlai
Chu Teh	Zhu De
Kiangsi	Jiangxi
Kuomintang	Guomindang
Li Ta-chao	Li Dazhao
Lin Piao	Lin Biao
Liu Shao-chi	Liu Shaoqi
Mao Tse-tung	Mao Zedong
Peking	Beijing
Peng Teh-huai	Peng Dehuai
Shensi	Shaanxi
Tien An Men	Tiananmen
Tsunyi	Zunyi
Yenan	Yanan

1893	Mao is born on December 26 in Shaoshan in Hunan province.
1911	Mao enlists in the revolutionary army during China's Republican Revolution.
1921	Mao helps found the CCP (Chinese Communist Party).
1923–1927	First United Front: Nationalist Party (NP) and CCP cooperate to defeat warlords.
1927	Mao writes report stressing revolutionary potential of Chinese peasants.
1927	NP leader Chiang Kaishek turns on the Communists in April. Mao leads unsuccessful Autumn Harvest Uprising and flees with a small army to Jinggangshan in Jiangxi province.
1928–1931	Mao merges forces with Zhu De, establishes Jiangxi Soviet.
1934–1935	Long March of Red Army from Jiangxi Soviet to Shaanxi province.
January 1935	Zunyi Conference brings Mao leadership of CCP.
1936–1946	Mao at Yanan base in Shaanxi province
1937–1945	Sino-Japanese War; Second United Front of CCP/NP
1946–1949	Civil War: Communists ultimately defeat Chiang Kaishek
1949	People's Republic of China is proclaimed by Mao on October 1 in Beijing.
1950	Chinese-Soviet Treaty of Friendship and Mutual Alliance
1950–1953	Korean War
1958	Great Leap Forward begins.
1959	Mao breaks with Defense Minister Peng Dehuai and replaces him with Lin Biao.
1966–1969	Great Proletarian Cultural Revolution
1969	Border clashes between Soviet Union and China
1971	Lin Biao dies after his alleged conspiracy to topple Mao is revealed.
1972	Mao meets with U.S. President Richard Nixon in Beijing.
1976	Mao dies on September 9, 1976, in Beijing at the age of 82.

CHAPTER 1

1. Quoted in Ross Terrill, *Mao Zedong: A Biography*. Rev. ed. Stanford: Stanford University Press, 1999, p. 198.
2. Quoted in Philip Short, *Mao: A Life*. New York: Henry Holt, 2000, p. 419.
3. Quoted in Jonathan Spence, *Mao Zedong*. New York: Penguin, 1999, p. 75.

CHAPTER 2

4. Quoted in Edgar Snow, *Red Star over China*. Rev. ed. New York: Grove Press, 1968, p. 136.
5. Ibid., p. 143.
6. Quoted in Shu Guang Zhang, *Mao's Military Romanticism: China and the Korean War, 1950–1953*. Lawrence: University Press of Kansas, 1995, p. 25.
7. Quoted in Short, *Mao*, p. 94.
8. Ibid., p. 84.
9. Ibid., p. 102.

CHAPTER 3

10. Ibid., p. 171.
11. Quoted in Spence, *Mao Zedong*, p. 75.
12. Ibid., p. 75.
13. Quoted in Zhang, *Mao's Military Romanticism*, p. 14.
14. Ibid., p. 14.
15. Zhang, p. 18.
16. Bevin Alexander, *How Great Generals Win: The Brilliant Maneuvers and Military Strategies That Won Wars and Built Empires—and the Men Who Planned Them*. New York: Avon, 1993, p. 188.
17. Quoted in Short, *Mao*, p. 222.
18. Quoted in Zhang, *Mao's Military Romanticism*, p. 19.

CHAPTER 4

19. Quoted in Short, *Mao*, p. 254.
20. Quoted in Alexander, *How Great Generals Win*, p. 191.
21. Quoted in Short, *Mao*, p. 222.
22. John R. Elting, *The Superstrategists: Great Captains, Theorists, and Fighting Men Who Have Shaped the History of Warfare*. New York: Charles Scribner's Sons, 1985, p. 244.
23. Quoted in Short, *Mao*, p. 286.
24. Ibid., p. 296.
25. Quoted in Alexander, *How Great Generals Win*, p. 196.
26. Quoted in Elting, *The Superstrategists*, p. 246.
27. Quoted in Short, *Mao*, p. 12.
28. Terrill, *Mao Zedong*, p. 127.
29. Ibid., p. 156.
30. Quoted in Snow, *Red Star over China*, p. 455.

31. Quoted in Terrill, *Mao Zedong*, p. 156.
32. Alexander, *How Great Generals Win*, p. 203.
33. Terrill, *Mao Zedong*, p. 166.
34. Ibid., p. 166.
35. Shaun Breslin, *Mao*. New York: Longman, 1998, p. 32.
36. Quoted in Ibid., p. 32.

CHAPTER 5

37. Quoted in Short, *Mao*, p. 339–40.
38. Elting, *The Superstrategists*, p. 250.
39. Quoted in Zhang, *Mao's Military Romanticism*, p. 23.
40. Ibid., p. 24.
41. Ibid., p. 24.
42. Quoted in Short, *Mao*, p. 255.
43. Quoted in Zhang, *Mao's Military Romanticism*, p. 14.
44. Quoted in Short, *Mao*, p. 367.
45. Ibid., p. 392.
46. Ibid., p. 392.
47. Ibid., p. 414.
48. Quoted in Spence, *Mao Zedong*, p. 107.
49. Ibid., p. 107.
50. Quoted in Zhang, *Mao's Military Romanticism*, p. 20.
51. Harrison E. Salisbury, *The New Emperors: China in the Era of Mao and Deng*. Boston: Little Brown, 1992, p. 58.
52. Quoted in Short, *Mao*, p. 418.

CHAPTER 6

53. Terrill, *Mao Zedong*, p. 202–3.
54. Quoted in Jian Chen, *Mao's China and the Cold War*. Chapel Hill: University of North Carolina Press, 2001, p. 88.
55. Quoted in Salisbury, *The New Emperors*, p. 113.
56. Spence, *Mao Zedong*, p. 118.
57. Terrill, *Mao Zedong*, p. 236.
58. Salisbury, *The New Emperors*, p. 134.
59. Quoted in Breslin, *Mao*, p. 98.

CHAPTER 7

60. Quoted in Terrill, *Mao Zedong*, p. 306.
61. Quoted in Salisbury, *The New Emperors*, p. 212.
62. Quoted in Spence, *Mao Zedong*, p. 161.
63. Breslin, *Mao*, p. 130.
64. Quoted in Terrill, *Mao Zedong*, p. 357.
65. Spence, *Mao Zedong*, p. 174.
66. Quoted in Salisbury, *The New Emperors*, p. 371.
67. Quoted in Short, *Mao*, p. 419.

Alexander, Bevin, *How Great Generals Win: The Brilliant Maneuvers and Military Strategies That Won Wars and Built Empires—and the Men Who Planned Them.* New York: Avon, 1993.

Breslin, Shaun G., *Mao.* New York: Longman, 1998.

Chen, Jian, *Mao's China and the Cold War.* Chapel Hill: University of North Carolina Press, 2001.

Cowley, Robert and Geoffrey Parker, eds., *The Reader's Companion to Military History.* New York: Houghton Mifflin, 1996.

Elting, John R., *The Superstrategists: Great Captains, Theorists, and Fighting Men Who Have Shaped the History of Warfare.* New York: Charles Scribner's Sons, 1985.

Embree, Ainslie T., ed., *Encyclopedia of Asian History.* New York: Charles Scribner's Sons, 1988.

Hutchings, Graham, *Modern China: A Guide to a Century of Change.* Cambridge, MA: Harvard University Press, 2000.

Li, Zhisui, *The Private Life of Chairman Mao.* New York, Random House, 1994.

MacKerras, Colin, ed., *Dictionary of the Politics of the People's Republic of China.* New York: Routledge, 1998.

Marrin, Albert, *Mao Tse-tung and His China.* New York: Viking, 1989.

The New Encyclopaedia Britannica. 15th ed. Chicago: Encylopaedia Britannica, 1998.

Salisbury, Harrison E., *The New Emperors: China in the Era of Mao and Deng.* Boston: Little, Brown, 1992.

Short, Philip, *Mao: A Life.* New York: Henry Holt, 2000.

Snow, Edgar, *Red Star over China.* Rev. ed. New York: Grove Press, 1968.

Spence, Jonathan, *Mao Zedong.* New York: Penguin, 1999.

Terrill, Ross, *Mao Zedong: A Biography.* Rev. ed. Stanford: Stanford University Press, 1999.

Zhang, Shu Guang, *Mao's Military Romanticism: China and the Korean War, 1950–1953.* Lawrence: University Press of Kansas, 1995.

Dunster, Jack, *China and Mao Zedong*. Cambridge: Cambridge University Press, 1982.

Fritz, Jean, *China's Long March: 6,000 Miles of Danger*. New York: Putnam, 1988.

Marrin, Albert, *Mao Tse-tung and His China*. New York: Viking, 1989.

Snow, Edgar, *Red Star Over China*. Rev. ed. New York: Grove Press, 1968.

Stefoff, Rebecca, *Mao Zedong: Founder of the People's Republic of China*. Brookfield, CT: Millbrook Press, 1996.

Web Sites

"Mao Zedong" by Jonathan D. Spence, *Time*'s Leaders & Revolutionaries
http://www.time.com/time/time100/leaders

"Modern China," Washington State University World Civilizations
http://www.wsu.edu:8001/~dee/MODCHINA/MODCHINA.HTM

LOUISE CHIPLEY SLAVICEK received her master's degree in history from the University of Connecticut. She is the author of five other books for young people: *Life among the Puritans, Confucianism, Women of the Revolutionary War, Israel,* and *Juan Ponce de León*. She lives in Columbus, Ohio, with her husband, Jim, a research biologist, and their children, Krista and Nathan.

CASPAR W. WEINBERGER was the fifteenth secretary of defense, serving under President Ronald Reagan from 1981 to 1987. Born in California in 1917, he fought in the Pacific during World War II then went on to pursue a law career. He became an active member of the California Republican Party and was named the party's chairman in 1962. Over the next decade, Weinberger held several federal government offices, including chairman of the Federal Trade Commission and secretary of health, education, and welfare. Ronald Reagan appointed him to be secretary of defense in 1981.

During his years at the Pentagon, Weinberger worked to protect the United States against the Soviet Union, which many people at the time perceived as the greatest threat to America. He became one of the most respected secretaries of defense in history and served longer than any previous secretary except for Robert McNamara (who served 1961–1968). Today, Weinberger is chairman of the influential *Forbes* magazine.

EARLE RICE JR. is a former design engineer and technical writer in the aerospace industry. After serving 9 years with the U.S. Marine Corps, he attended San Jose City College and Foothill College on the San Francisco Peninsula. He has devoted full time to his writing since 1993 and has written more than forty books for young adults. Earle is a member of the Society of Children's Book Writers and Illustrators and the League of World War I Aviation Historians and its sister organization in the United Kingdom, Cross & Cockade International. He belongs to the United States Naval Institute and the Air Force Association.